summits to reach

SUMMITS TO REACH

An Annotated Edition of Franklin Rhoda's

REPORT ON THE TOPOGRAPHY OF THE SAN JUAN COUNTRY

Edited and with Preface by Mike Foster

Published through the assistance of
the Harold McBride Memorial Fund of
the Colorado Mountain Club Foundation

PRUETT *P* PUBLISHING COMPANY
Boulder, Colorado

First Edition

1 2 3 4 5 6 7 8 9

Printed in the United States of America

Library of Congress Cataloging in Publication Data
Rhoda, Franklin.
Summits to reach.

  Bibliography: p.
  Includes index.
  1. San Juan Mountains Region (Colo. and NM.)—
Description and travel. 2. Mountaineering—
San Juan Mountains (Colo. and N.M.) 3. Rhoda,
Franklin. I. Foster, Mike, 1935-   . II. Title.
F782.S19R48 1984 917.88'38042   84-15135
ISBN 0-87108-667-0 (pbk.)

This book is for
Bonnie Hardwick and Louisa Ward Arps

CONTENTS

ILLUSTRATIONS

EDITOR'S PREFACE

As we should not judge a book by its cover, we should not ignore Rhoda's essay because of its title. Hidden behind his overly modest and rather bland menu awaits a rich banquet that rewards sampling.

Some of Rhoda's delicacies have been justly celebrated, such as his lightning storm atop Sunshine Peak, or his daring first ascents of Uncompahgre Peak, Mount Sneffels, and Mount Wilson. Sadly, only connoisseurs have tasted these treats, for after enjoying popularity immediately after its publication in 1876, the *Report* promptly went out of print. The time has come to retrieve Rhoda's chef d'oeuvre from the deepfreeze, and to announce that event with a foretitle more suitable to the man and his work; hence, *Summits to Reach: Report on the Topography of the San Juan Country.*

Written by a brilliant twenty-year-old just a year out of college, the *Report* is an accurate account of a surveying party in Colorado during the summer of 1874. In the process of mapping some 5,200 square miles of perhaps the most rugged and scenic part of the Rocky Mountains, Rhoda and his colleagues fended off grizzly bears, barely escaped electrocution several times, and observed the first prospectors in the mining camps. They climbed thirty-five summits over 12,000 feet, most of which had never been ascended. Trails were few, roads even rarer, and reliable guides nonexistent. Unsettled Indian relations made the possibility of being attacked very real.

Fully aware of the unique experiences enjoyed—or endured—by his comrades, Rhoda fashioned a minor literary masterpiece. Out of the ingredients of daily camp life and the mixed blessings of exploring a wilderness, he prepared a feast whose main entries include mountaineering, alpine scenery, dramatic weather, scientific exploration, and encounters with wildlife.

The author never complains of bugs, dirt, bruises, getting lost or disoriented, the aggravation of false summits, or the

1

frustrations of jungle-thick timber. Even four days of rain cannot dilute his enthusiasm. Nor does he admit to fatigue, despair, homesickness, anger, or fear. Anyone in the wilderness for a prolonged time endures hardships and has sour moments. Rhoda chose to turn his adversities into a humorous and insightful account of a government expedition. And why not? After all, he was having the time of his life.

As a stylist, Rhoda reflects his era in one way, and in another he departs from it. His turn of a phrase, though often captivating, is decidedly Victorian. On the other hand, while most writers of his time described nature according to strict rules, which forced varying landscapes into stereotyped formulas, Rhoda found original expression by relying on his own acute perceptions. In short, he gives us his personal experience, and in that sense, too, he was a pioneer.

Rhoda came to Colorado as a member of the Hayden Survey, officially called the United States Geological and Geographical Survey of the Territories, directed by Ferdinand Vandeveer Hayden during the years 1867–79. Hayden's Survey was the forerunner of the United States Geological Survey, organized in 1879. His Survey studied geological formations, collected samples for scientific research by botanists, biologists, zoologists, and paleontologists (among others), and climbed mountains. From these high points, or stations, topographers and geologists coordinated their knowledge of the country, enabling them to compile maps in Washington during the winter. Beginning in the summer of 1873, Rhoda worked for three years in Colorado. Then, and for the remainder of his life, Rhoda found many summits to reach.

Because of the cornucopia Rhoda delivers, it may seem peevish to disclose the gaps in his narrative. On the other hand, these omissions give employment to his editor. An awareness of some of those things Rhoda took for granted, or chose to abbreviate, or could not have known, can only add to our enjoyment of the whole. Who would have guessed, for example, that the leader of the party, Allen D. Wilson, was Rhoda's half brother? The close bond between these two very different men influenced in subtle ways nearly every page of Rhoda's *Report*, which in a sense is a paean to an idolized older brother. I

2

have told of their intertwining lives in the Biographical Notes, following the text, but let me sketch the three main characters of Rhoda's lively but mostly impersonal *Report*.

Wilson was a born leader and outdoorsman who before coming to Colorado with Hayden in 1873 had mastered alpine surveying with the Geological Survey of California and the Fortieth Parallel Survey. He had also climbed Mount Ranier and explored widely in the Pacific Northwest. In later years he went on to become chief topographer for the USGS, charter a bank, and make a fortune. His clear eye and common sense inspired trust, and during a crisis he was the kind of man others wanted to follow.

Rhoda, too, became a leader, the kind who takes dead aim on your heart, and whose actions stir up strong feelings. Rhoda's life was a religious quest, full of controversy. Even as an undergraduate he gave warning of his calling, and before his thirtieth birthday he had organized a Sunday school and launched a crusading newspaper. With equal fervor he railed against the producers of wealth, which was ironic considering that his father's money gave him the independence to fulminate against mammon. Eventually he calmed down sufficiently to become a Presbyterian minister, in which capacity he served several parishes in California for over thirty years.

Rhoda, Wilson, and the geologist Fred Endlich worked together for three seasons in the field, until they finished their assignment in southern Colorado. Personality conflicts may have distracted other groups, but this trio was known for hard work and no fuss. That surprised me at first. Not only was there the volatile Rhoda to contend with, but in piecing together the men's characters I came to know Endlich as a somewhat haughty and intolerant man who could work up a good temper. That he and Rhoda both stayed in line I attribute to the towering integrity of Wilson. At thirty, Wilson was by a few years the oldest of the three, and his plentiful ability, along with an already enviable reputation, made him a powerful natural leader. All this by way of saying that Wilson's example inspired the best in Rhoda.

The others in the San Juan division remain shadow figures: a negro cook, two packers (one identified only as Ford, the

3

other not at all), and a "general assistant," C.E. Gallup, who, Hayden reports, made barometric observations.[1] Gallup probably gathered data at fixed points, like Saguache and Del Norte, but almost certainly did not accompany the field party.

Hayden also explained why he sent Wilson's party to pioneer the exploration of southwestern Colorado in 1874: "In 1873, the tract of land supposed to contain all or nearly all of the metalliferous lodes was purchased from the Ute Indians by the United States Government. It was therefore one of the main objects of the San Juan Division to inquire into the geological and mineralogical characteristics of these lodes, with a view to obtain some idea regarding their relations and value."[2]

Rhoda says little about people met along the way, though he does refer to miners here and there. Undoubtedly, the group ran into very few others in this unexplored land. That also explains his indifference to towns: precious few yet existed. He met settlers just in the act of organizing Lake City and Silverton, and he found established towns at Saguache, Howardsville (just north of Silverton), Animas City (Durango), and Del Norte. He passed through the future locations of Telluride, Rico, and Creede, but in 1874 disturbed neither prospectors nor ghosts.

It is somewhat surprising Rhoda records no encounters with Indians. One wonders if he were trying to hide something, because in the annual report for the next year, William Henry Holmes (another geologist) states that "in 1874 Mr. Wilson's party had been ordered back by them [the Utes]."[3] Actually, Rhoda would have had no reason to hide any such meeting; on the contrary. Others in the field freely described the red man when seen, and had the opportunity presented itself Rhoda's sharp eye would not have been caught napping. I can only assume that the party saw no Indians, and that Holmes misunderstood what Rhoda says on page 86 about the Utes chasing homesteaders away from Animas City.

---

[1] *Eighth Annual Report of the Geological and Geographical Survey of the Territories* (Washington, 1876), p.9.

[2] *Ibid.*, p. 10.

[3] F.V. Hayden, *Ninth Annual Report*, p. 238.

4

Concerning the technical aspects of editing, I have wanted to add clarity and points of interest without breaking the flow of the adventure. But at times Rhoda needs editorial assistance. He was careless about chronology. His sometimes vague references set up verbal roadblocks. Then, too, through no fault of his, some names and spellings have changed.

To make generous but unobtrusive use of the editorial privilege, I have adopted three rules: (1) brackets in the text provide spelling variants of proper names, clarifications and corrections of a word or two, and a regular, corrected chronology; (2) footnotes at the bottom of the page supply emendations and insertions no longer than a line, including cross references to maps; (3) endnotes develop the historical context, identify individuals, and add longer remarks and corrections. Only the most necessary additions, therefore, appear on the pages of the text itself, while longer comments reside in a location not distracting to a reader wishing to recreate the pace of the original.

Because it would be annoying to repeat spelling variations like Howard[s]ville, and demeaning of contemporary usage to reiterate continually Mount Aeolus [Eolus], I have elected to show such modern variants in brackets only at the initial instance. On the other hand all name changes—the White Earth [Cebolla Creek], or Godwin [Henson] Creek—are repeated at each occurrence.

Capitalization and punctuation (except for a few obvious typos) remain as Rhoda left them. His paragraphs wander like pack trains, however, and I have broken up a number into more topical blocks to simplify reading. All his figures for distance and elevation have been faithfully preserved, though notes indicate where he strays from current standards by more than a mile horizontally or one hundred feet vertically.

The Appendix discusses fully the topographical stations. The maps on pp. 144-49 give a bird's-eye view of all fifty-four stations. Readers requiring more detail—for example, to retrace Rhoda in the field—should obtain the County Map Series of Colorado. I used that Series because it is the most recent issued by the USGS, and its scale (1:50,000, or about 1¼ inches to the mile) permitted me to follow Rhoda on only twelve different sheets. In footnotes I have noted the route's progression from the first of those sheets to the last. "La Plata 3 to Hinsdale 2," for example, means movement from the third La Plata County sheet to the second Hinsdale County Sheet.

Only two printings of Rhoda's *Report* have been done. The first appeared in Hayden's *Bulletin of the United States Geological and Geographical Survey of the Territories*, Vol. I, 2d. Series, No. 3 (May 1875), pp. 165–209; the second in Hayden's *Eighth Annual Report* for 1874, published in 1876. The second version adds material in the last three paragraphs, inserts additional phrases in two other places, and makes several stylistic changes here and there without altering the sense of the first. For these reasons I used the second printing as the standard text. Rhoda's two topographical sketches in this edition, however, appeared only in the first printing. Both the first and second printings contained a statistical appendix, which I chose not to include in this edition.

In opening up the path for Rhoda's return from obscurity, I have had a lot of help. First I want to thank those who accompanied me for part of the summer of 1982, while retracing and studying Rhoda's route: Peter Dessauer, Kathy Hoerlein, Jerry Bensema, Bob Vos, Mel and Sarah Ryan-Roberts, Henry Hare Foster, and especially Elaine Carlson, who also served as my botanical and geological advisor. I marched with a light load because Lougene Baird dehydrated all my food. I located all the stations largely because Dudley Tyler Smith loaned me his copy of Hayden's *Atlas of Colorado* (1881). Mike Wolfe's research on historic surveying practices enabled me to see the country through the eyes of a nineteenth-century topographer. And all the while I was away from home my garden blossomed because of generous neighbors, Marge Underwood and Lois Ryan.

During the field work a number of people took a spontaneous interest in the idea. I have forgotten none of them, but I can name only Terry and Marie Chamberlain, Dan and Robin Lockerby, Allison Paulsen, Graham and Susan Phipps, Don and Jolene Stott, also the several owners of private property who permitted me access, and the two anonymous families from Arlington, Texas and (I know not where) Tennessee, who took pity on an unkempt hitchhiker with a bad case of blisters.

Doing research reminds me that librarians are probably civilization's best hope. It is a sincere pleasure to acknowledge the courtesy of those who work at the Bancroft Library, the Alameda County Courthouse, the Huntington Library, the Denver Branch of the National Archives, the Presbytery of San Francisco, the U.S. Cartographic Information Service (Denver), the USGS Field Record Office in Denver, the public libraries of Denver, Los Angeles, and Oakland, and the university libraries in Boulder, Laramie, and Berkeley.

Special assistance came from Grace E. Baker (The Society of California Pioneers), Patrick Carroll (California Banking Commission), Teresa Hickey (Bank of America), Michael D. Peterson (San Francisco Theological Seminary), Mary Plummer (Presbyterian Historical Society), and Judy Sheldon (California Historical Society).

One of the high points of my research was meeting members of Rhoda's family. This happened through the Fruitvale Presbyterian Church, Oakland, where Rev. Jerry Van Marter joyfully encouraged me to study the records of Rhoda's pastorate there, which began eighty-five years ago. Rev. Van Marter introduced me to Sybil Wangburg, who then told me how to reach Rhoda's daughter, Grace Dahlstrom, who in turn, after giving me a splendid personal interview, put me in touch with her own daughter, Mrs. Gerald J. Vieira. Pauline taught me more in a day about the idiosyncrasies of her grandfather than I had learned in a year's study. She also dug up several of Rhoda's published articles found nowhere else and generously copied them for me.

Rev. Jim Kitchens brought out the records of another parish, the First Presbyterian Church of Oakland. Back home, I got useful remarks from writing colleagues Bill Bueler, Mel Griffiths, Jim Norland, and Bob Ormes—three of whom are mountaineers. Bueler and Ormes persuaded the U. S. Board on Geographic Names to designate a summit in Rhoda's honor. Mount Rhoda (13,402 feet) rises four miles southeast of Silverton. Kathlene Sutton and Joe Martin insisted I stay with them during outings to Laramie. Cia Wenzel helped with proofreading, and the Colorado Moutain Club Foundation made a timely grant from the Harold McBride Memorial Fund.

Coincidence makes any enterprise more memorable, and I discovered a number of such fortuities. Rhoda and Endlich shared the same birthday. Hayden was forty-six when he brought his Survey to Colorado in 1873; I was the same age 109 years later when I set out to follow Rhoda in the field. Rhoda's nickname and my legal given name are the same, Frank. Rhoda's half brother helped him become a skilled topographer; my half brother, Melvin Sowles Ryan-Roberts, assisted in making me a passable photographer, and he reproduced some of the pictures for this book. The lady who looked over Rhoda's shoulder as treasurer of the board of trustees at Fruitvale Presbyterian for years was a Miss Hardwick, the same name as my own guardian angel at the Denver Public Library, Bonnie Hardwick, who has watched over and encouraged my progress from the start. It all began when Bonnie and Louisa Arps both insisted that Rhoda deserved a wider audience. I had just begun gathering materials for a biography of Hayden and was surprised to learn Louisa had once assembled a similar collection. She turned over her Hayden file to me and suggested I work back to him by getting to know Rhoda first. I still cherish that advice.

Report on the Topography of the San Juan Country

Pioneer Surveyors of the San Juan Mountains: Fred Endlich (standing), Frank Rhoda and A.D. Wilson posed for William Henry Jackson in September 1874 near Howardsville—*Courtesy USGS.*

REPORT ON THE TOPOGRAPHY
OF THE SAN JUAN COUNTRY

By Franklin Rhoda, Assistant Topographer

In the following report I have adopted the very common system of describing the country in the order of our travels through it. The system is a very faulty one, but seemed to be the best possible under the circumstances. In describing a river or a simple range of mountains, the order of sequence is laid down in nature; all you have to do is to commence at one end of the line and follow it. The mountains in the so-called San Juan country, however, are very complicated, and present no definite lines that may be followed in a description without leaving much untold. They appear, not in a single range, nor in a succession of ranges, but as a great mass. It was thought best to intersperse here and there in the description of topography such personal adventures of members of the party as might throw light on any features of the country or its climate.

We started from Colorado Springs on the 14th of July, 1874, taking the road leading up the Fontaine qui Bouille [Fountain Creek], and over Ute Pass into South Park. It would have been much shorter to have gone to Pueblo by rail, and thence on horse or mule-back around the southern end of the Greenhorn [Wet] Mountains, through Huerfano Park and Mosca Pass, and across San Luis Valley to Del Norte. But at this time of the year we knew that along the low plains the heat would be intense and the grass and water scarce. As it was we had a delightfully cool trip all the way, with plenty of grass for our animals. Our road lay across South Park, thence down the Arkansas River and across the range at Puncho [Poncha] Pass into the San Luis Valley.

We reached Saguache on the 24th of July,[1] and made inquiries of different persons as to the nature of the country for which we were bound; but although they were all deeply interested in the prospects of the new mines, nobody could give us any definite information. We could not even find out

11

whether the country was made up of rugged mountains or only high plateaus. Two days after leaving this place we reached the Los Pinos agency, where the Southern Utes receive such supplies as are apportioned to them by the Government. This point was in the extreme southwest corner of the district surveyed in 1873, and was the point of beginning the past summer.[2]

Our first station was made [July 27] on a peak which had been occupied in 1873 as station 34.* It is a low point, a few miles northwest of the agency, and is less than 12,000 feet in elevation. Having a most beautiful day, and plenty of time at our disposal, we found it very pleasant to study the country that appeared in the southwest, in which our summer's work was to be. We could see none of the very rugged masses of mountains which beset our path and taxed our energies in the months following. What did appear to us was as follows: A little to the west of south, and not more than fifteen miles distant, rose up the high group in which station 33 of 1873 [Stewart Peak] was situated, and containing several peaks ranging in height from 13,500 to near 14,000 feet.[3] Farther around to the west, but much more distant, appeared a high pyramidal-shaped peak, which is situated south of the Rio Grande, and is marked on the map as Rio Grande Pyramid. A little farther to the right, and still more distant, was a double-topped peak, afterward occupied as station 23, and named Mount Oso. Still farther around, another distant, high peak appeared to be the culmination of a high mountain mass; this is Mount Aeolus [Eolus] on the map.[4] Nearly in the same direction, but much nearer, there appeared a high plateau, extending over many degrees of the horizon.[5] Being more than twenty miles distant from us, and lying wholly above timber-line, it was a very interesting feature in the landscape. At our distance it seemed to be covered with grass; but this we after-ward found was not the case. Our subsequent experience showed us that in this part of the country these high super-timber-line plateaus are very common. Immediately beyond this area was a high mass of red-colored mountains, afterward

---

*Saguache County Map, Sheet 1.

12

the scene of some interesting electrical experiences.* A few miles northwest of this group Uncompahgre Mountain [Peak] appeared, presenting on its north side the peculiar precipice which distinguishes it from all the surrounding peaks. North of this a series of ridges and plateaus extends from the high mountains to the Gunnison River.

Having made profile sketches of the mountains and drainage sketches of the water-courses in the vicinity, and having taken angles to every prominent peak, bluff, and stream junction visible, we started for camp.[6] The next morning [July 28] found us on our way to the great San Juan country, of which we had heard so much and found out so little. Our course at first lay to the southwest, along the Ute trail, which leads from Los Pinos [Creek] over to the Rio Grande.** We ascended one of the peaks [station 2] in the small group containing station 33 of the previous season, and had a good view of the deep and rugged cañons leading outward from the center of the mass.

In the several succeeding days [July 31-August 1] we made stations 3, 4, and 5 on the high plateau already mentioned. From this plateau we got the grandest view of Uncompahgre obtained from any station during the summer.[7] The full height of the great precipice stood out in clear profile. Its striking resemblance to the profile of the Matterhorn gave us a wholesome dread of it, for as yet it had never been ascended by any one, and we felt that to reach the summit might be beyond the range of the possible. The plateau upon which we stood ranges in elevation from 12,400 to 12,700 feet above the sea, and covers an area of about 15 square miles. We rode over it on our mules, to make the station[s], and found it covered with loose rock, which in some places was so rough as to necessitate long detours in going from one point to another. As in many other cases which occurred subsequently, we found this plateau covered with puddles of water, and wherever there was soil it was always boggy. On the west and north sides it was terminated by bluffs, ranging in height from 1,000 to 2,500 feet, the last 200 to 500 feet being nearly vertical. On

---

*Sunshine Peak and Redcloud Peak.
**Saguache 1 to Hinsdale 1.

13

Wilson and Rhoda on Station 25. Wilson triangulates with the theodolite while Rhoda makes profile and drainage sketches—*Courtesy USGS, W.H. Jackson, 1874.*

the west side of the plateau the bluff terminates below in rolling, timbered land, which extends a little over a mile to the bed of Lake Fork. The total fall from the top of the bluff to the stream is 4,000 feet, in a horizontal distance of one and a half miles.

Having finished this part of the country, we traveled down the White Earth [Cebolla Creek]* to the point at which it emerges from the upper cañon [August 2 & 3]. Here the new road from Saguache[8] crosses it at a small angle, and, swinging far up to the north to avoid the high bluffs, it finally turns up Lake Fork at a point about twelve miles from the crossing of the White Earth [Cebolla Creek]. Thence our course lay up stream, and we traveled [August 4 & 5] along just west of our plateau stations and nearly under the bluffs.** From a camp just below the junction of Godwin [Henson] Creek and Lake Fork we made station 8 [August 6] on a point about five miles east of Uncompahgre Peak.[†]

The next station to be made was on the great peak itself. In order to accomplish this, it became necessary to move [August 7] with our pack-train about five miles up Godwin [Henson] Creek, to a point where it is joined by a small stream coming in from the north.[††] Leaving the train at this point, and taking an extra mule with us to carry our blankets and food, we rode with great difficulty up the side gulch, and camped at an elevation of 11,900 feet, near the timber-line. We started out early the next morning [August 8], expecting to have a very difficult climb. We were terribly taken aback, however, when, at an elevation of over 13,000 feet, a she grizzly, with her two cubs, came rushing past us from the top of the peak. Contrary to all expectations, we found the ascent very easy, and arrived on the summit at 7:30 a.m., having been two hours and a half in climbing up 2,400 feet. We found that the bears aforesaid had been all over the summit of the peak, though how they got up over one or two short but steep pass-

---

*Hinsdale 1 to Gunnison 6.

**Gunnison 6 to Hinsdale 1.

[†]On Crystal Peak.

[††]Nellie Creek.

ages in the ascent, puzzled us not a little.

The summit of the mountain is quite smooth, and slopes from the brink of the great precipice toward the south. It is composed of several successive flows of lava, in horizontal position, which gives it a stratified appearance, and causes the slope to the south to appear terraced in profile. On the north the edge is sharp and definite, and the precipice so perfectly vertical, that by dropping a stone a few feet from the edge it fell 1,000 feet before striking an obstacle, as we determined by timing the descent. The bluff surrounds the peak on all sides except the narrow strip on the south end, and is about the same height all around, but not so nearly vertical as on the north side.[9]

From here, for the first time, we were able to see the great massiveness of the mountains in our district. To the south the peaks appeared in great numbers, and in the distance appeared a group of very scraggy mountains, about which the clouds were circling, as if it was their home.* Subsequently we found that they were most of the time thus enveloped. The high mountains near us covered the horizon from the east around by the south to the west. Nearly due west of us appeared a very high, sharp peak, which was afterward ascended as Mount Sneffels, and just to the south of it another high mass, bearing in its center a large, flaring patch of snow. The culminating point of this was, later, station 35, or Mount Wilson. Southeast of us, and about eight or ten miles distant, was a mass of peaks, filling the whole space between Lake Fork and Godwin [Henson] Creek, all of a bright red color.[10] The highest of these points is over 14,000 feet above the sea. Ten or fifteen miles to the southwest was another smaller mass of lower peaks of the same color, while in various places appeared mountains of white, yellow, and blue, all the colors being very well defined and clear.[11] They were caused by the oxidization of iron and other ingredients of the rocks. To the north the mountains fall very suddenly down to the bed of the Gunnison; in fact, the peak is situated on the extreme north line of the Uncompahgre Mountains.[12]

---

*Mount Eolus and neighbors. See note 30.

16

Just before we left the summit, clouds came along, and we were soon enveloped. It was at this time that we experienced, for the first time in the season, the electrical phenomena which later interfered so much with the topographical work. As at this time these phenomena were not very marked, and as our experience on all the peaks was very similar, the detailed account of them is reserved for another place. We made the entire descent that evening from the summit to Godwin [Henson] Creek, where the pack-train had left us, getting the benefit of a rain before reaching camp.[13] Up to the second day before this the weather had been very fine, but from this time till fall, rain commenced early every afternoon, and continued into the night.

Moving up Godwin [Henson] Creek, Dr. Endlich made a special examination of some of the highly-colored peaks already mentioned, while Wilson and I rode up [August 9] to the head of the cañon and out upon a high and pretty extensive plateau, which extends from a high, sharp pinnacle a few miles west of Uncompahgre Peak around the heads of Godwin [Henson] Creek and Lake Fork to the head of the Animas. It forms the divide between these three streams and the Uncompahgre River.[14] An area of fifteen or twenty square miles is above the timber-line. Ten or fifteen square miles have an elevation of over 12,000 feet. The timber-line here ranges from 11,500 to 11,900 feet above the sea. This whole area is covered with a very short growth of grass, which is almost entirely unfit for feed for animals. This is common with all the grass growing high up on the mountains; it is not nutritious.

Unlike the plateau east of Lake Fork, this is not surrounded by bluffs. Instead of being smooth and nearly level, like the former, it is rolling and cut up by gulches. The slopes down to the surrounding streams are steep, but bluffs are very rare. The ground is not very rocky, but like all the soil at this elevation, is very damp and boggy. A number of small lakes are dotted here and there over it, and in many places springs of ice-cold water gush out from the rocky prominences, fed by the banks of eternal snow which are scattered about in considerable numbers. In crossing this elevated region a strong west wind was blowing, and, the temperature being below the freezing-point, riding was very disagreeable both for our beasts and ourselves. Under these circumstances we were not so observant as we should otherwise have been. Still, there were so many new and interesting things about us that we could not fail to notice some of them.

The eastern half of the plateau drains out through a cañon* leading northward and westward into the Uncompahgre River.** We crossed its head on our tramp, and noticed that it fell very suddenly, till within about two miles of us it became a deep, narrow cañon, at which point the stream turned abruptly to the west. From this fact we were enabled to get a good broadside view of the north bluff of the cañon, and we saw it weathered out most curiously, being worn into almost all conceivable fantastic shapes, the general appearance being that of a great wall covered with niches and statuary. Time would not permit us to go closer and make a more careful examination; so we had to content ourselves with a distant view. From the headwaters of this creek we crossed a divide[+] running laterally across the plateau, and for some distance the drainage was into Godwin [Henson] Creek, until, near the peak upon which we made our station, the water again flowed to the north.[++]

From station 10 [August 10] the cañon of the Uncompahgre River appeared in all its ruggedness. From here we got a fine view of Mount Sneffels and its surroundings. We could see no possibility of ascending the peak from the east side, as it was cut up by rugged cañons and innumerable bluffs and pinnacles; these latter ornamenting all the ridges leading down from the great peak and its near neighbors.

In some places numbers of the pinnacles massed behind one another presented the appearance of church-spires, only built after a much grander style of architecture than most of our modern religious edifices. In some places two systems of vertical pillars were separated by a narrow strip of horizontal

*Either Cow Creek or Wildhorse Creek.
**Hinsdale 1 to Ouray 2.
[+]Ouray 2 Hinsdale 1.
[++]Hinsdale 1 to Ouray 2.

lava-flow, and served to heighten the fantastic appearance of the rock-forms. The fact that we stood on a peak four or five miles distant from the scene described, will give some idea of the great size of these pinnacle-forms.[15] A month later we had another much nearer and finer view of this same curious group from a peak several miles southwest of us.* Beyond this we saw nothing of interest that cannot be better described in the sequel.**

The next day [August 11] found us retracing our steps down Godwin [Henson] Creek. After camping a night at the junction, we moved up Lake Fork [August 12], making a station by the way on a low point near the stream.† A few miles above the junction we came to a beautiful lake bearing on Mr. Prout's[16] map the name "San Cristoval." [San Cristobal] This is by far the finest of the many little lakes we saw during the summer. It is in the bed of the cañon, and has been formed by a slide from the east side of the stream. Judging from the growth of pines over this slide we concluded that it had taken place in very recent times, but how recent we could not determine.[17] The lake is about one mile and a half in length, and in some places as much as a quarter of a mile in width. Several very small islets covered with willows add much to the beauty of the scene. A thick growth of pine timber surrounds it on all sides. To the east there is a tolerably easy slope back to the foot of the bluffs of the high plateau. On the west side the high mass of red mountains rises abruptly from the water's edge.

It was near the lower end of this lake that the Randolph party of artists discovered the bodies of five men the day after we passed them at this point. They are supposed to have been murdered by white men for their money.[18]

The cañon of Lake Fork is nowhere so rough as that of Godwin [Henson] Creek, and the trail is quite good for the greater part of the distance to the head of the stream. After camping a short distance above the lake, and getting a good night's rest, we took an early start on one of the most curiously

---

*That is, from station 29.
**Ouray 2 to Hinsdale 1.
†Station 11, east of Lake City.

interesting and strangely dangerous trips of the season [August 13]. We had to ride up the creek several miles before making the ascent of the peak for which we were traveling. From this fact we were thrown late and got caught on the summit in one of the afternoon storms. Intermingled with other unusual drawbacks, we had a fair share of the common but not less disagreeable climbing over loose rocks and through fallen timber; neither were events of the chase wanting to add to the great variety of incidents encountered during this eventful day.

The object in view was to make a station on the highest point of the red mass above mentioned.[19] In order to accomplish this, we had to follow up a ridge, along which patches of loose rock alternating with timber made the riding very difficult. It soon became impossible to follow the ridge any farther, and we had to cross the gorge on our left, going down 300 or 400 feet, and up again more than a thousand feet to the summit of the next ridge. Riding was out of the question, so we had to lead our mules. After getting out of the cañon the ground became smoother, and near the timber-line we rode along without difficulty, the land being very open and covered with grass. It was here that a considerable herd of mountain-sheep appeared in the distance. We saw them before they saw us, and, leading our mules out of sight, slipped through the timber with the utmost care; but before we could get in position the sentinel of the herd, posted on a prominent point, gave the alarm, and they all instantly took to flight. Wilson succeeded in shooting one on the run. As we had had no fresh meat for two weeks, the result of the shot was very gratifying to us all.

For the rest of the ride the ground was covered with a short growth of grass, but devoid of trees, as we had passed the timber-line. At an elevation of 13,000 feet the soil ended abruptly, and from that point on, all was loose rock. Here we hitched our mules to stones, and, taking the notebooks and instruments, continued the ascent on foot. This part of our work was quite easy, although the height we had to climb was nearly a thousand feet vertical. Before reaching the summit of the first high point on the ridge, we noticed stray clouds wandering up and down the neighboring cañons, as if only waiting for us to reach the top before commencing the attack.

Seeing that it would be impossible to reach the main peak before the storm would burst upon us, we made our station on the first point. The main peak is 41 feet higher and a mile and a half distant, being connected with it by a long unbroken ridge. Had time permitted, we should probably have occupied both points as stations, but we were unfortunately prevented from doing this by the peculiar circumstances to be described. Station 12 [Sunshine Peak], the southern and lower of these two points, is situated in the upper bend of Lake Fork, where, from flowing in a southeasterly direction, it swings around to the east. Near the base of the peak Lake Fork receives its principal tributary from the south side, which on Mr. Prout's map bears the name of Snare Creek.[20] This peak is the most southerly of the red group included between Godwin [Henson] Creek and Lake Fork. Its height is 13,967 feet above the sea. On the north and east sides the slopes are quite steep but regular, while on the south and west the sides are very precipitous, with a fall from the summit to the valley below of 4,400 feet in a horizontal distance of one mile.

On arriving at the summit, Mr. Wilson hastily made a rough sketch of the surrounding drainage, and then set up the instrument,* while I proceeded to make a profile sketch of the mountains south and west of us.[21] We had scarcely got started to work when we both began to feel a peculiar tickling sensation along the roots of our hair, just at the edge of our hats, caused by the electricity in the air. At first this sensation was only perceptible and not at all troublesome; still its strength surprised us, since the cloud causing it was yet several miles distant to the southwest of us. In the early part of the storm the tension of the electricity increased quite slowly, as indicated by the effect on our hair. By holding up our hands above our heads a tickling sound was produced, which was still louder if we held a hammer or other instrument in our hand. The tickling sensation above mentioned increased quite regularly at first, and presently was accompanied by a peculiar sound almost exactly like that produced by the frying of bacon. This

---

*The theodolite. See note 6.

latter phenomenon, when continued for any length of time, becomes highly monotonous and disagreeable. Although the clouds were yet distant, we saw that they were fast spreading and already veiled many degrees of the horizon. As they approached nearer, the tension of the electricity increased more rapidly, and the extent of our horizon obscured by them increased in nearly the same ratio; so that the rapid increase in the electric tension marked also an increased velocity in recording angles and making sketches. We felt that we could not stop, though the frying of our hair became louder and more disagreeable, for certain parts of the drainage of this region could not be seen from any other peak, and we did not want to ascend this one a second time.

As the force of the electricity increased, and the rate of increase became greater and greater, the instrument on the tripod began to click like a telegraph-machine when it is made to work rapidly; at the same time we noticed that the pencils in our fingers made a similar but finer sound whenever we let them lie back so as to touch the flesh of the hand between the thumb and forefinger. This sound is at first nothing but a continuous series of clicks, distinctly separable one from the other, but the intervals becoming less and less, till finally a musical sound results. The effect on our hair became more and more marked, till, ten or fifteen minutes after its first appearance, there was sudden and instantaneous relief, as if all the electricity had been suddenly drawn from us. After the lapse of a few seconds the cause became apparent, as a peal of thunder reached our ears. The lightning had struck a neighboring peak, and the electricity in the air had been discharged. Almost before the sound reached us the tickling and frying in our hair began again, and the same series of phenomena were repeated, but in quicker succession, at the same time the sounds becoming louder.

The clouds now began to settle into the Great Cañon of the Lake Fork, and boiled about in a curious manner; here and there a patch of cloud would separate from the main mass and move about by itself. In passing over a thick cluster of pines down near the bed of the cañon, the lower parts would get caught and drag through with the greatest seeming difficulty. The different parts seemed to be affected by different currents in the air, and at times two little masses of cloud would pass each other less than a mile apart, but would soon turn aside, or rise up, or lose themselves in the great cloud that pretty nearly filled the Great Cañon and its branches. At times a portion of the mass, moved by an upward current, would rise several hundred feet above the general level, and, the force ceasing, would topple over and slowly fall back and lose itself in the general mass. The whole moved about in a chaotic manner, producing a curious effect. When you consider that the top of the cloud was not less than 2,000 feet below us, you can form some idea of the strange scene that presented itself to our eyes in those exciting times.

The clouds soon began to rise up and approach us. As they did so, the electricity became stronger and stronger, till another stroke of lightning afforded instantaneous relief; but now the relief was only for an instant, and the tension increased faster and faster till the next stroke. By this time the work was getting exciting. We were electrified, and our notes were taken and recorded with lightning speed, in keeping with the terrible tension of the stormcloud's electricity. The cloud reached us, coming on like a fog, looking thin and light near us, but densely white at a short distance. All the phenomena before mentioned increased in force after each succeeding stroke of lightning, while the intervals between strokes became less and less. When we raised our hats our hair stood on end, the sharp points of the hundreds of stones about us each emitted a continuous sound, while the instrument outsang everything else, and even at this high elevation could be heard distinctly at the distance of fifty yards. The points of the angular stones being of different degrees of sharpness, each produced a sound peculiar to itself. The general effect of all was as if a heavy breeze were blowing across the mountain. The air was quite still, so that the wind could have played no part in this strange natural concert, nor was the intervention of a mythological Orpheus[22] necessary to give to these trachytic* stones a voice.

Having completed a rough sketch of as much of the sur-

---

*Volcanic.

rounding country as was not obscured by clouds, I hastily took up the mercurial barometer, hoping to get a reading before we should be compelled to leave the summit; but, alas! too late for success.[23] The lightning-strokes were now coming thicker and faster, being separated by not more than two or three minutes of time, and we knew that our peak would soon be struck. As I took the barometer out of its leather case, and held it vertically, a terrible humming commenced from the brass ring at the end, and increased in loudness so rapidly that I considered it best to crawl hastily down the side of the peak to a point a few feet below the top, where, by lying low between the rocks, I could return the instrument to its case with comparative safety. At the same time Wilson was driven from his instrument, and we both crouched down among the rocks to await the relief to be given by the next stroke, which, for aught we knew, might strike the instrument which now stood alone on the summit. At this time it was producing a terrible humming, which, with the noises emitted by the thousands of angular blocks of stone, and the sounds produced by our hair, made such a din that we could scarcely think. The fast-increasing electricity was suddenly discharged, as we had anticipated, by another stroke of lightning, which, luckily for us, struck a point some distance away.

The instant he felt the relief, Wilson made a sudden dash for the instrument, on his hands and knees, seized the legs of the tripod, and flinging the instrument over his shoulder dashed back. Although all this occupied only a few seconds, the tension was so great that he received a strong electric shock, accompanied by a pain as if a sharp-pointed instrument had pierced his shoulder, where the tripod came in contact with it. In his haste he dropped the small brass cap which protected the object-glass of the telescope; but, as the excitement and danger had now grown so great, he did not trouble himself to go back after it, and it still remains there in place of the monument[24] we could not build to testify to the strange experiences on this our station 12. We started as fast we we could walk over the loose rock, down the southeast side of the peak, but had scarcely got more than 30 feet from the top when it was struck. We had only just missed it, and felt thankful for our narrow escape.

We could not follow down the ridge we came up, as, in the present state of affairs, it was highly dangerous to cross any prominent point, even though it should be much lower than the peak itself. Hail and sleet began to fall freely, and as we descended to a lower level they were exchanged for rain, with which we were well drenched, even before reaching the mules.

We found Dr. Endlich waiting for us, having just returned from the ascent of a lower point of the main peak, where he had experienced similar phenomena to those already described, only differing from them in degree. He said he had seen the lightning strike our peak, and at first thought that we might have been caught, till finally he saw us coming down the mountain.

Our mules seemed glad to see us, not because they cared one straw for us personally, but because our arrival was the signal for the return to camp. Whether they had been pestered by the electricity, we could not tell, but they were doubled up into the most compact shape that mules are capable of assuming, and did not seem to appreciate at all the romance connected with a cold rain-storm at a high altitude.

Hastily putting on the saddles, we started down the mountain-side. By this time the clouds enveloped us entirely, and rain fell almost without intermission till long after we reached camp.

On our way we loaded one of the mules with the meat of the sheep killed on our way up, but as it was a very difficult matter to tie the whole animal securely across the saddle, it gave us a great deal of trouble, as in going down steep places it would slip forward, and in going through brush it would be pulled back. To go back the way we came was such a very difficult task that Wilson concluded to take a short cut for camp, though this involved the risk of coming to bluffs or impassable slides. We had to lead our mules the whole way, which was very steep, and composed of loose rock mixed in among the thin, straight stems of the quaking-asp* trees. Here and there we came to large patches of loose *débris* without

---

*Aspen.

any trees, and were compelled to fall back and take a new tack. The rain was still falling heavily when the sun set and darkness commenced.

In these high altitudes there is scarcely any twilight, and darkness quickly follows sunset. I will not go through all the details of our descent, as nothing occurred beyond what has happened in the experience of every mountain-climber. We reached camp late in the night, thoroughly drenched, and had to eat supper in the rain, which was anything but pleasant [still August 13].

If I could end the history of the adventures of this remarkable day by describing how we were pleasantly housed in dry, comfortable quarters, and how we contentedly "wrapped the drapery of our couch about us and lay down to pleasant dreams," I would. But, alas! how the romance would be taken out of the story if I should tell how we crawled into our low, short, and narrow little tents, with the water running under at the edges, and leaking through at the top, and how we had to lie as still as possible lest we might disturb the pools of water gradually collecting on our blankets, and precipitate them into the inner recesses of our bed clothes.

All this and more shall I leave untold, and cease to disturb the several members of the party, placidly snoring away in the babe-like innocence of their slumbers. And while they thus replenish their wasted energies with the nocturnal balm of sleep, may the unwearied mind of the reader wander like a restless ghost up and down this interesting cañon, and observe with care the high and picturesque walls of trachyte which extend from the creek-bed to the summit of ever-memorable station 12, and wonder, it may be, at the pine-trees scattered here and there in the cracks in the rock, 2,000 feet above him, having scarce a root-hold, and looking so diminutive as to suggest the idea that some Japanese had been there and applied their wonderful art to stunt them to their apparent pigmy stature. If, too, he extends his observations up the scarcely less imposing cañon of Snare [Cottonwood] Creek, he will find many more things wonderful in their nature, but too varied to find a place in such a hasty sketch as this.

If the reader, after having satiated his curiosity with the

"Dog Tents" offered poor shelter for two men and their gear—*Courtesy American Heritage Center, University of Wyoming, W.H. Jackson, probably 1875.*

many wonders of nature here laid out before him, will return from his wanderings to the camp he left the night before, an interesting scene will soon present itself to his eyes. If, a little before the break of day, he observe closely the tents of the several sleepers before mentioned, he will soon observe a movement in the one occupied by our huge black cook.[25] That little circumstance marks the dawn of the next fiscal day, even though the first object emerging from the tent be as black as night. In all countries it is a recognized fact that the darkest part of the night comes just before the dawn, and the present case tends to confirm the truth of the adage. The morning is bright and clear, but all things not under close cover are wet, and wood is no exception to the rule. The cook searches about under trees and bushes till he has collected together an armful of tolerably dry branches, and then makes the fire. The fire burns, and another era in the cook's existence has commenced. He takes four sheet-iron pots, all of different sizes, and starts for the creek. A man of less muscle would content himself with two. He soon returns with all the vessels filled with water, and places some of them on the coals to heat, one for the coffee, the others for cracked wheat, hominy, or other articles.

At this stage of the proceedings there is some commotion in another tent, and presently the two packers emerge from their cover fully equipped for the day. One immediately starts out to hunt up the mules, while the other puts the packs and aparejos* in order. The cook proceeds to bake his bread in a Dutch oven,[26] while the rest of the party still snore on. In the intervals of his cooking he opens the mess-boxes, sets them about four feet apart, opens out the leaves, and, placing a support under the middle, spreads his cloth, and the table is ready. A short time before everything is ready he rings the first bell for breakfast, by yelling out, in the barbarous mountain dialect, "Grub pile!" or sometimes simply "grub," for short. At this there is great commotion, and the rest of the crew "pile out" in all sorts of shapes and in all states of nudity. They hurry for there is no driver like hunger, and they now feel a yearning in the inner man that cannot be repressed, and

---

*A special pack-saddle.[27]

their love of sleep itself gives way. A general rush for the nearest water soon takes place. In a few seconds all are washed, and immediately commence the attack on the breakfast-table. They make short work of it, and at 7 o'clock all are in their saddles and off.

Following the trail [August 14] up the creek [Lake Fork], we found it very rough, but at a point west of station 12 the bed of the cañon widened out, and from there our riding was quite easy. Leaving a notice on a tree near this place, for the train to encamp, we ascended a low peak to the south and west of the creek [station 13]. From this point we succeeded in clearing up some points in the topography which had been unavoidably missed from station 12. Two miles west of it was a very high, massive mountain, with a great horizontal band of white running across the face of a high bluff on the northeast side of the peak. This mountain bears on the map the name of Handie's[28] [Handies] Peak, and was ascended the day after this as station 14.

From station 13 we had a splendid view of the red mass to the north and east, station 12 being the nearest of all the peaks. The last 2,000 feet in height was composed wholly of dull-red *débris*, with very few bluffs. Here appeared some of the finest mountain forms any of us had ever seen. From our distance, which was several miles, the individual stones were all lost to the eye, and the slopes appeared as if they were made of red sand, but of course having the forms which naturally result from coarse *débris*. The tops of the ridges were nowhere jagged, but were invariably formed of gracefully-flowing curves, while mountain-lines could scarcely be more beautiful than the magnificent sweeps of the curves formed by the long *débris* slides. Except on the south and west sides of station 12, these curves were nowhere broken by any considerable bluffs. Having reached this station early in the morning, we were not troubled with storms during our work.

Several large silver-bearing veins crossing the ridge near this station gave us the first intimation of our approach to the mining region. We descended to camp, which we found just at the base of the peak, and arrived quite early in the afternoon.

The next day, August 14[15], we moved up stream, leaving

directions with the packers where to make camp. We rode up a small creek coming in from the south,* which drains the basin between station 13 and Handie's Peak. The ground most of the way was very miry, and the brush and timber very difficult to pass through. After passing the timber-line, the only difficulties in our way were the boggy ground and rocks. One or two very steep slopes, along which we had to ride, were very disagreeable; but much less so for us than for the poor donkeys. At an elevation of nearly 13,000 feet we found a grassy patch of ground, which was large enough and level enough for our mules to stand on without much danger. Having secured them to the rocks, we climbed up the peak, which we found a very easy matter, as the total rise was scarcely a thousand feet and the slope quite gentle. A short distance below this summit, at an elevation of about 13,500 feet, we found some shallow prospect-holes sunk on a vein which cut transversely across the ridge. As yet we had seen none of the miners, but these holes, with accompanying notices written on a stake, indicated their presence somewhere in the vicinity.[29] We soon reached the summit of Handie's peak, and found it not near so acute as most mountain-summits in this region. This peak is very massive, with high bluffs on the east side, which continue along the east ridge around to station 13. Between the two stations is a deep basin, amphitheatrical in form. To the south and west the slopes are steep, but not precipitous.

To the west, and several thousand feet below us, we saw several little lakes of a bright emerald-green color. We had no opportunity to make any investigations as to the cause of the color, but from observations later in the season we concluded it must be due to vegetation at the bottom of the lakes. The white band already mentioned as appearing on the east bluff was found to be composed of volcanic ash. Here, again, we saw a band of sheep, but having left our guns at the mules we could not shoot them.

Early in the day we noticed the clouds hovering about the quartzite peaks, as we had seen them so often before.[30] They

*Grizzly Gulch, their route up Handies Peak.

30

THE QUARTZITE GROUP, SAN JUAN MOUNTAINS

THE LA PLATA MOUNTAINS

Two Drawings by William Henry Holmes. Holmes' view of the "Quartzites" (top) is from the east; Jackson's (Fig. 10) and Rhoda's (Fig. 15) are from the west. From Hayden's *Atlas of Colorado* (1881)—*Mel Ryan-Roberts, 1983.*

31

never completely veiled all the peaks of the group, but early each day began to circle about them in a restless sort of a way, like so many mighty lions about their lair. To us this apparent restlessness suggested a consciousness of their terrific destructive power, which only awaited a mandate from the "God of storms" to be set in motion.[31] We even now held those peaks in awe, as there seemed to be established somewhere in their midst a regular "manufactory of storms." Our subsequent experience among them never completely obliterated this idea. About 1 o'clock in the afternoon the clouds again came on, accompanied by hail and electric phenomena similar to that previously described. We could detect the electricity in the air long before the clouds reached us by holding our hands high in the air, when a faint clicking was audible.

The phenomena were precisely similar to those experienced on station 12, but having reached the summit earlier in the present case, we were able to leave before it became very dangerous. Just before leaving the top I slung the strap of the tripod over my shoulder, and experienced a sharp pain at the two points where the tripod touched me. Otherwise the phenomena were much the same as on the previous station. This peak is 13,997 feet above the sea, and 30 feet above station 12. After[wards], the hail and rain commenced, and fell incessantly till far into the night.

The following day [August 16] we crossed the pass from the head of Lake Fork to the Animas.* The elevation of this pass is 12,540 feet. The ground up to that point is very boggy and the riding disagreeable. The rise in the last mile of distance is more than 1,000 feet. How the people of Saguache ever expect to bring a wagon-road up this I cannot see. On account of the surrounding bluffs there is very little opportunity to wind the road up it, while the miry nature of the soil will require vast sums of money to be spent after the grade is obtained before the road can be made passable.[32] The fall from the pass down to the Three Forks of the Animas [Animas Forks] is very sudden.

Leaving the train to proceed to Howard[s]ville, wherever

---

*Cinnamon Pass. Hinsdale 1 to San Juan.

that might be, we climbed up a peak on the north side of the trail. This point commands the headwaters of the Animas, and is 13,675 feet in height.[33] We succeeded in getting a few of the most necessary details of the topography, but as we had traveled a considerable distance since morning, it was late before we reached the summit, and about the usual time the electric storms again commenced. By this time the romance connected with these phenomena had all disappeared; and at this time and thereafter, whenever our hair began to fry, we generally disappeared at pretty short notice. We never waited again so long as we had done on station 12.

As we were working on the peak, peculiar sounds reached our ears from the depths of the Animas Cañon, 2,500 feet below. They resembled very much the whistle of a locomotive when heard from a great distance. By listening carefully and looking through our glasses, we formed a shrewd surmise that this strange sound was the last indrawn note of the plaintive bray of the jackasses used by the miners in bringing the ore down from the mines. The harsh lower notes had all been dissipated before they reached us, leaving nothing but the refined essence of the sound behind. We considered this as a conclusive evidence of the presence of white men, and immediately descended to our mules.

The trail down to the Animas was quite steep, notwithstanding it wound around a great deal. For the last part of the distance the fall was very sudden down to the Three Forks [Animas Forks]. The total fall from the pass is 1,400 feet in two miles. At what is called the Three Forks [Animas Forks], or the junction of the three creeks which form the head of the Animas, we found several cabins with a number of miners about, who kindly showed us specimens of ore from their various mines. As Dr. Endlich will give a detailed description of the mines, I will refer the reader to his accompanying report.

A very short distance below the forks, the great bluffs of the Animas Cañon commence, at first more or less broken up by slides and by gorges formed by streams from the mountains. A little while after leaving the forks the trail crosses the Animas, and follows across the great rock-slides which come down to the water's edge on the east side of the stream. These extend many hundred feet above the trail, and are terminated above by a series of high bluffs, one receding behind the other and separated usually by small *débris* slides, similar to the great one below; sometimes very steep grassy slopes form the connection between the bluffs. Above all, a long slope, more or less steep, connects the last and highest with the mountain-peaks above, which are from 3,000 to 4,000 feet above the stream-bed, but seldom ever visible from the trail, as the near precipices cut off the view. The bluffs on the west side are for a long distance much less broken than on the east, and instead of having slopes at their bases, rise abruptly from the bed of the cañon, in many places a thousand feet, nearly vertical. But the series of perfectly inaccessible bluffs often rise from 2,000 to 3,000 feet above the stream, and are connected with the mountain-peaks by steep grassy or rocky slopes. In some places the bluffs form the abrupt termination of what from above are seen to be sharp, rocky ridges, leading down from the peaks. In the upper end of the cañon the only gorge cut through the western wall is that of Eureka Gulch . Near its junction with the Animas this is very narrow, but a short distance back it widens out into a considerable basin.

A very interesting thing in connection with these bluffs is the fact that many little streams run over the top and reach the bed of the cañon by a succession of little falls. These give a picturesque appearance to these otherwise bare bluffs.[34] Still more important is their bearing on questions connected with the working of the mines. A fall of from 1,000 to 2,000 feet could be easily obtained. It can scarcely be doubted that there is a never-failing hydraulic power contained in these little streams sufficient to work all the machinery that can ever be brought into these mines. All that is required is to apply it properly. In making this general assertion, I do not refer simply to those streams which fall over the bluffs of the main cañon of the Animas, for it must be remembered that, up Cunningham, Arastra [Arrastra], and other gulches, there are hundreds of other similar streams that can be used just as well, if not even better than these.

While crossing the great slide on the trail, we could see miners at work against the bluffs on the west side of the river.

Curious-looking zigzag trails led up to these mines. Others were tunneling from the bed of the stream, and seemed to be in a poor position in case of a great spring-thaw, as all of their work would then be wasted. At one place we saw an ice-bridge over the stream, which struck us as a novelty, for the middle of August, at an elevation of only 10,000 feet, in this latitude.

At a point about five miles below the Three Forks [Animas Forks] the steep slide across which we were riding abruptly ended, and we came out into a thick clump of trees in which were several log cabins, bearing on a flaring sign-board the word "Eureka," evidently intended for the name of a town that was expected to be, though what had been found here to suggest the name was not immediately apparent. It is not impossible, however, that the first settler coming up the Animas here found his farther upward progress barred by the great rock-slide. At this point the bed of the cañon suddenly widens out to a quarter of a mile or more in breadth, forming the upper end of Baker's [Bakers] Park.[35] A great portion of the level ground is here covered by willows and swale grass, cut through and through by old beaver-ditches. After leaving Eureka, the ground is very uneven, and quite devoid of timber, except up the sides of the cañon.

The bluffs on the west side become more and more precipitous, and less broken up by gorges; while on the east the few bluffs which presented themselves farther up stream are exchanged for steep rocky mountain-slopes, with few bluffs. At a point about three miles below Eureka the Animas is joined by Cunningham[36] Creek, a considerable tributary, coming in from the east side.

Howardville,[37] containing at the present time some eighteen or twenty log cabins, is situated on both sides of this stream near its mouth. This is the first settlement in Baker's Park, and among its other attractions can boast of a store, a butcher-shop, assay-office, shoemaker-shop, and post-office. Although as yet there is no regular mail-communication with the outside world, it is expected that a regular mail-route will soon be established by the Post-Office Department. All mail is now brought in from Del Norte by occasional travelers, and letters cost ten cents besides the regular United States postage.[38]

Howardsville—*Courtesy USGS, W.H. Jackson, 1875.*

From this position a splendid view of some of the silver-veins can be obtained. The face of the high bluffs, west of the town and across the river, is covered with a net-work of yellow veins, extending from the bed of the stream up as far as we could see. Later we found that these same veins cropped out on the other side of the mountain, individual veins being continuous the whole distance. We found some of them crossing the highest point of the ridge at an elevation of 13,500 feet, thus giving a vertical depth for the outcrop of 3,800 feet, while the horizontal distance was not less than the thickness of the ridge, a length of from three to four miles. How much farther they may have extended horizontally, we could not make out in our limited time.

At a point nearly west of Howardville the bluffs end, and steep grassy and rocky slopes take their place and continue to the lower end of the park.

On August 16[17], the day after our arrival at the town, we crossed the river and ascended a peak northwest of Howardville, but not quite visible from that place on account of the intervening bluffs. The slopes were all grassy, but so steep that we could ride but a small part of the distance. We came upon the top of the ridge near a little sharp point on the spur, which I believe is the one designated by the name of "King Solomon's Mountain."[39] Just a little below the top of this point we found a level patch of ground about 20 feet square, where we concluded to leave our mules, as such level places seemed to be rare in this vicinity. Looking about, we saw only one stone of sufficient size to hitch our animals to, and that was an oval one; but as no alternative presented itself, we tied the ropes of the two mules together, and then fastened them as well as we could to the stone. The result of this will be seen on our return.

The main peak was about half a mile to the north of us, but as the ridge was easy to walk over, we had little difficulty in reaching the top. On this peak we made station 16. Its elevation is 13,541 feet, as determined from the mean of twenty-three readings with a mercurial barometer. This point is not very sharp, but is simply the culminating point of several rocky ridges. From here a splendid view of the vicinity of

Baker's Park may be obtained, although only a small part of the park itself is visible. In order to understand rightly the situation and peculiar position of this very interesting park, it will be necessary to give now a general description of it, leaving the minor details to be filled in in our future travels. From this point we can see nearly the whole of the great depression of which Baker's Park forms the most important part.

Just to the east of us the Animas runs along, its deep cañon nearly 4,000 feet below our present position, but the high bluffs bordering on the west succeed in completely hiding the stream from view. Howardville is also shut out from the sight by the same obstruction, although it almost comes within the field of view. The fall from the summit of this peak to the stream near Howardville is 4,000 feet in 9,500 horizontal.* Just across the river, Galena Mountain has a fall to the Animas of 3,700 in a horizontal distance of 7,000 feet,** while down to the nearest point on Cunningham Creek, the fall is 3,500 feet in 5,000 feet horizontal.[40] On the southwest side of Cunningham Gulch the fall is even greater than this. These cases are not unusual specimens, but I have selected them because the peaks are well known and can be easily found on the map. I could instance many others where the fall was full as great and even greater. From station 16 we had a good view up Cunningham Gulch, from the fact that the continuation of the direction of the stream passed almost exactly through the station.

Along the east side of the Animas a line of high peaks extends, from its head down to the lower end of the great cañon, a distance of thirty miles.[41] At the north end of the line, but draining into Lake Fork, is Handie's Peak, with an elevation of 13,997 feet. Next come two nameless peaks, the first having an elevation of 13,830 feet[+] and the second 13,770 feet[++] above the sea; then Galena Mountain, with an elevation of 13,290 feet, and next, Mount Kendall,[42] 13,380 feet above sea-level. Below this for some distance lower points continue

---

*Closer to 11,000 horizontal.

**More like 10,000.

[+]Jones Mountain.

[++]Niagra Peak.

the chain, till we come to the group of quartzite peaks, ranging in height from 13,600 to 14,054 feet, where the line culminates in Mount Aeolus and Pidgeon's [Pigeon] Peak, and, falling off suddenly to the south, soon loses itself in the plains of Southern Colorado and New Mexico.

The great and important feature of this region is the far-famed Baker's Park. Small in area and quite unimportant in itself, it would be utterly disregarded if situated in other parts of Colorado; but, located as it is, surrounded on all sides by the most rugged mountains in the Territory, if not in the whole Rocky Mountain system, this little area of flat land becomes an object of curiosity and interest. When looked at as the center of the great mining district, it becomes an object of great practical importance. But not till one has crossed over the several passes leading out of it can he feel a proper regard for this little spot, so carefully guarded by nature from the invasion of man. In itself, it is nothing more than the bed of the deep cañon of the Animas, spread out at the lower end to a width of a mile or two. It extends from the little town of Eureka, already mentioned, down the Animas to the base of Sultan Mountain, a distance of about nine miles. It is divided into two parts, the upper of which is contained between Eureka and Howardville, a distance of about three miles, and is quite rolling, so much so as to be scarcely worthy the name of the park. Below Howardville the cañon again contracts till within about three miles of the base of Sultan Mountain, when the cañon-bed widens out into a beautiful level piece of land, about three miles long, in the direction of the stream, and having a width of from one to two miles. It contains, in all, from 2,000 to 3,000 acres. This is the true Baker's Park; but the division between the two portions, as we have described them, is not important, and in nature not well-defined. The wide part above Howardville tapers almost insensibly into the narrow part below it, but the line between this narrow part and the true park below is quite definite.

The new town of Silverton,[43] at present containing about a dozen houses, is situated near the center of the level area, on the south side of Cement Creek, a stream flowing into the Animas from the west,[44] and passing through the park. Bounding Baker's Park on the south is Mineral Creek, which, flowing from the west, highly impregnated with iron, sulphur, and other ingredients, hugs closely the foot of Sultan Mountain, and joins the Animas near the entrance of the lower or Great Cañon. Almost all the water in this country is as pure as any in Colorado, but this stream is so strongly impregnated with mineral ingredients as to be quite unfit for drinking. The elevation of Silverton is 9,400 and of Howardville 9,700 feet. From our present position, looking down the valley, it seems to be completely closed up by Sultan Mountain, and the exit of the river is not visible.

At the lower end of the park the Animas swings around toward the southeast, and for about seventeen miles[45] cuts a most terrific cañon, ranging in depth from 2,000 to 4,500 feet in depth, through quartzite rock almost as hard as steel.[46] It might have been expected that in the beginning the stream would have selected its course somewhere near the junction of the trachyte and sandstone with the quartzite. It seems, however, to have been turned by some agency another way, and so cut its course through the harder rock this long distance, without being at any point more than three miles distant from the softer material.[47]

In order to get a true conception of the isolation of Baker's Park from the rest of the world, a thorough understanding of the passes leading out of it is necessary. First, let me say that the ruggedness of the great Cañon below the park is such that travel through it must long be a matter of great difficulty, though it is said that some miners have passed up from the plains on the south into Baker's Park by that route.[48] The trail at present most traveled by persons passing between Baker's and Animas Parks crosses over the southeast slope of Sultan Mountain. At the divide this trail has an elevation of 10,460 feet, but the highest point is several hundred feet higher than this. This route is the roughest and most dangerous of any leading out of the park, and even in the best summer weather is unsafe for pack or riding animals.[49]

The next pass is the one on the southwest side of Sultan Mountain, which has an elevation of 11,570 feet above the sea, and, though not dangerous like the preceding, is very disagree-

Bakers Park and Modern Silverton. Anvil Mountain dominates the view north from the southeast slope of Sultan Mountain—*Mike Foster, 1982.*

41

able, from the bogs, fallen timber, and rock-slides which beset one's way.[50]

Another is the Bear Creek [South Fork] Pass, leading from the head of Bear Creek [South Fork] to the head of the San Miguel, on the west side of the mountains. Its elevation is 12,600 feet.[51] On the east a long stretch of fallen timber in a bog, through which the trail passes, makes travel very difficult. On the west a great rock-slide, over which the trail leads, is scarcely less disagreeable.

Two passes lead over to the head of the Uncompahgre River, but, as the box-cañon of the latter bars all egress, they require no description here.[52]

To the east of our present position are the two passes at present mostly used by persons passing to and from the mines. The first, from the head of Lake Fork to the head of the Animas, having an elevation of 12,540 feet, has been already described.* The other, the pass from Cunningham Gulch to the Rio Grande, has an elevation of 12,900[12,090][53] feet at the highest point of the trail.[54] Over this has passed almost everything that has been brought into the park. The trail is very steep, and in the best weather is muddy, and after a rain it becomes perfectly horrible.

When it is remembered that the height of a great part of the park is only 9,400 feet, it will be seen that the ascent from the valley to each of the five passes at present used will be, in feet, as follows: 1,300, 2,200, 3,200, 3,140, and 2,690.[55] This gives some idea of the way this little valley is isolated from the outside world. This, then, is the far-famed park, named after that daring leader of his little band, who lost his life within its bounds.** This is the *cul de sac* into which he and his men were mercilessly driven by the Indians in 1862 [1868]. How many fell in the massacre, how many starved or froze to death, seems even yet to be veiled in mystery. But how the present survivors ever escaped might well remain a mystery when we consider the great depth of snow that must then have covered these high mountain-passes, and that, at that

---

*Cinnamon Pass.

**See note 35.

date, the country was perfectly unknown.

From our station 16 only the lower end of the park, including Silverton, is visible. The view of the mountains, however, is very extensive, all the high peak stations made up to this time being plainly visible, except the first one south of Los Pinos agency [i.e., station 2]. Mount Sneffels stands out boldly, about fifteen [thirteen and a half] miles to the northwest of us, while about an equal distance to the east [seventeen miles to the southeast] of us appears the high peak, called, from its shape and location, the Rio Grande Pyramid. Just a little east of south the quartzite peaks again stood out in their peculiar rugged-ness. From this point we also had a good view of Arastra Gulch.[56] Its upper end is a rocky amphitheater, between 12,000 and 13,000 feet in elevation. In its center was a little lake.* At the lower end of the amphitheater there is a very abrupt fall of from 1,000 to 2,000 feet down to the bed of the creek.

Having reached the summit of this peak unusually early, we had plenty of time to study the topography carefully. Just as we were finishing up the work of the station, and had commenced building a small monument out of the few stones in the vicinity, the well-known tickling sensation about the roots of our hair again commenced, and we could see its cause in the shape of a heavy rain-cloud which was slowly drifting up the cañon. We could see long dark streaks extending from the cloud to the valley below, indicating heavy rain. All rain-storms in this country, when seen from a distance, present this appearance. A continuous mist-like connection extends from the cloud to the earth, but through this are streaks much blacker than the rest. To a person unacquainted with those storms, these streaks would appear as bands of vapor, a little thicker than the rest. In truth, however, the part that seems like thin mist is heavy rain, while the black streaks are almost unbroken streams of water. These are what are usually known in the mountains as water-spouts. We left the summit before the electricity became very troublesome, but the rain which followed we could not avoid.

Packing up our books and instruments, we walked down

---

*Silver Lake.

to the place where the mules ought to have been, but where, to our amazement, they were not. Looking over the ridge, we saw the mules, still hitched together, standing on the steep east slope, about forty yards from the summit, but the round stone was nowhere to be seen. A heavy furrow through the snowbank, near the top of the ridge, with several deep indentations in the soil below, told a curious tale. It seems that as the storm came on, a strong cold wind arose from the west, which, with the accompanying rain, made the mules feel very uncomfortable, as they were on the west side of the ridge. In order to better themselves, they moved over to the other side, slowly dragging the stone after them, till, reaching the brink, the steep slope animated the otherwise inert stone with a considerable power, and it in turn took the mules in tow. Of course, as soon as they found themselves pulled they drew back, but, finding the stone inexorable, one of them moved up a step and found herself relieved of the strain, and commenced nibbling the short grass to be found in the vicinity. But what one gains the other loses. The whole weight of the stone now pulls on the second mule; but it is not in the nature of the beast to resist for a long time a steady and unrelaxing strain when unaccompanied by swearing. She moves a step forward, and, finding relief, goes to grazing. The first by this time has forgotten all about the stone, and, finding herself suddenly jerked, her whole asinine obstinacy is aroused, and she braces herself for resistance, but after a minute or so, finding the pulling force unaltered, and hearing no oaths proceed from the stone, she slowly comes to the conclusion that this is not a human contrivance, and moves up.

Thus by slow degrees the stone pulls them down the slope, over the little snow-bank and some distance beyond, disputing, of course, each step of the way, for such, alas! have we too often found, to our sorrow, to be the nature of the beast. After reaching a short distance from the top of the ridge, the rope evidently slipped off the stone, and the latter, rolling faster and faster, could have found no obstruction to its course for full 3,000 feet down feet down the mountain. What the mules themselves thought of their mysterious leader they never revealed; nor did we wait long in the cold rain to hear their story, but hurriedly putting on the saddles, dragged them down that mountain much faster than the stone did; but they moved on joyfully, for they knew as well as we that they were going to camp and to grass. Their shriveled forms and backs, curved up when we first found them, indicated clearly the fact that they were disgusted with the country, especially all of it above 13,000 feet in elevation. The rain now fell in torrents, and the grass being thoroughly wet, the walking was very disagreeable, but the slope was very steep and riding on our tired beasts very slow, so we walked most of the way and dragged our mules after us.

Reaching Howardville, Mr. Wilson found that the expected supplies had not arrived, so he concluded to finish the piece of country east of Howardville and down the Rio Grande as far as might be convenient.

The next day, August 18,[57] we started eastward up Cunningham Gulch, up which a well-marked trail leads over to the Rio Grande. This is by far the most interesting of the secondary cañons of the Animas system. After passing the main bend, which is about two miles east of Howardville, the side-slopes become steeper and steeper, and finally end altogether in becoming nearly vertical bluffs. These are nearly, if not quite, as high as those along the upper course of the Animas, already described. On the west side, these bluffs are rather more precipitous than on the east, and come down closer to the stream-bed. These consist usually of a series of bluffs one above the other, receding from the view. Over the last tier, which is from 1,000 to 2,000 feet above the stream, numerous small streams of water pour, and passing over the succeeding bluffs in falls and cascades present a beautiful spectacle. In the early spring, when the snow is melting and they are swollen to considerable streams, the sight must be magnificent.

A number of mines are located high up the slopes wherever they are not too steep to be ascended. Here and there a little low hut is visible on the east slope. Near the head of the gulch the trail is very muddy and badly cut up by travel. The upper part of the cañon ends abruptly with steep, high bluffs on all sides, except the narrow strip up which the trail winds to the pass. Several lodes are located at the head of the gulch. The amphitheatrical form of the head of the cañon with the great bluffs are very characteristic of volcanic formations, and all over the San Juan region they are the rule rather than the exception. Nevertheless, the sudden termination here of the great Cunningham Gulch is exceedingly interesting. The stream falling over these bluffs serves to heighten the effect.

The trail now leaves the creek and ascends the east slope. It is very steep and always muddy and slippery. The grade may be appreciated by calling to mind the fact that from the bed of the stream to the pass the rise is about 1,500 feet in one and a half miles horizontal.

The incessant travel over this trail by the miners, with their horses, mules, and burros, keeps it in a bad condition. Although it can scarcely be said to be dangerous, still its slipperiness adds much to the labor of the already overwrought beasts of the miners. The really bad part of the trail is only a small part of the whole distance. On the summit the ground is gently rolling, and the trail passes between low hills which form the principal part of the country in the immediate vicinity.* The elevation of the pass above the sea, as determined by a single reading of the mercurial barometer, is 12,090 feet.

We made station 17 on a table a short distance southwest of the pass. From this vicinity a good view of a number of the most rugged of the quartzite peaks may be had. Those that appear range in height from 13,600 to 13,800 feet.

After camping overnight on the head of the Rio Grande, the next day [August 19] we made station 18 on a peak between Pole and Lost Trail Creeks, whose elevation is 13,656 feet. From this peak we had a good view of the country south of Lake Fork. In this vicinity are scattered a number of pretty high peaks, but they are generally isolated from each other, and have none of the massiveness of the mountains about the head of Lake Fork and the Animas. In ruggedness they cannot compare with many that will be described further on. To the east the slopes begin to be more gentle, and at a distance of a few miles appears a pretty extensive plateau surrounded by high bluffs.

_____
*San Juan to Hinsdale 2.

The next day [August 20], in passing down the Rio Grande, we noticed a very peculiar formation consisting of a very bright-green colored rock weathered into little needles and spires. It is situated against the south side of station 18.

After camping near the junction of Lost Trail Creek with the Rio Grande, we made two stations on the high plateau, just to the east of the camp [August 21]. The climb was very difficult on account of the great masses of fallen timber we encountered and the bluffs that came in our way. Once on the top of the plateau, the riding was very easy. It was covered with loose rock (trachyte), but not so much so as to seriously impede our course. There being no prominent point, we were compelled to make two stations. No. 19 was made on the eastern part of the north edge, No. 20 on the west.

This plateau may be said to cover about five square miles; the elevation of most of this is over 12,000 feet. The eastern part slopes off quite gradually, while on the northwest and south the plateau terminates in nearly vertical bluffs which in many places are several hundred feet in height. To the east of this the ground becomes more and more even, till at a distance of about fifteen miles down the river Bristol Head rises abruptly to an elevation of 12,800 feet. From this position it appears in profile. From station 2, a series of high plateaus extends southward all above timber-line, and ranging in height from about 11,500 at the lowest point, a few miles north of Bristol Head, to about 13,000 feet, near station 2.[58] Southward from the lowest point, the plateau slowly rises till, after culminating in the bald summit of Bristol Head, it falls suddenly 4,000 feet down to the Rio Grande, and so terminates.

From station 19, a grassy slope, which we afterward found to be Antelope Park, seemed to extend to the bluffs of Bristol Head, but after looking with the field-glasses we saw that a cañon intervened. But look at it as much as we would, there was a peculiar appearance about it we could not then explain.[59]

From station 20 we had a splendid view of the Rio Grande Pyramid, which was eight miles distant, and across the river from us. This is probably the finest view that can be had of this beautiful mountain. Its pyramidal form is almost perfect, while at the same time there is just enough bluff intermingled with the *débris* slopes to give relief without the usual accompaniment of coarseness.

We left the plateau quite early, as we had a long distance to travel before reaching camp. The pack-train, according to orders, had traveled up the creek which comes into the Rio Grande from the south, a little below the mouth of Pole Creek.[60] We proceeded without a delay to follow them. At first the riding was quite easy. We passed several salt-licks, which were tramped full of tracks of deer and mountain-sheep. Soon the cañon narrowed in and traveling became very difficult. We found no trails, tracks, or signs of any kind to indicate that anybody had ever gone up the creek before us.

At several points the traveling was very dangerous; at one place that I now recall to mind it was especially so. The creek at that time was a considerable stream, and, from the great fall it had, was a perfect torrent. The bed was filled with large stones, and among these the water boiled and foamed terribly. At this point we had to slide our mules down a very steep, rocky slope of about 100 feet in height; at the bottom there was scarcely room enough for a man to stand conveniently between the slide and the stream. Just above this point was one of those deep pools where the big trout love to dwell, while at its lower end the water rushed through between several large rocks like a mill-race. Now the only way to cross was just at the lower end of the pool, where the water was shallow; below, the current was dangerously swift; above, the water was 6 or 7 feet deep.

Leaving the mules and instruments with me, Wilson scrambled across to the other side, and I threw him his mule's rope, and while he hauled I whipped the beast behind. After a few minutes of this treatment, with the asinine obstinacy for which this particular mule was famous, she leapt out into the pool and, swimming up the head, tried to climb up a smooth, wet rock, but did not succeed. After a thorough stoning she finally returned to me, and we repeated the experiment, this time with better success. Next, my mule, "Bones," was taken in hand. Having passed through the valley of humiliation the year before, and probably having taken mental notes on the disgraceful failure of her comrade's first attempt, she "made the riffle" with little trouble. Other experiences of a little less exciting nature served to heighten our dislike for this creek. Having climbed over 2,000 feet in the morning, and made two stations, we felt very tired, and our mules walked slowly.

After a while darkness began to come on, and camp did not appear. "Bones" began to take on that pitiful look engendered by her horror of having to stay out. Every time that such a contingency seemed probable her lower lip would fall and hang down in a strangely sorrowful way. She seemed to recall that awful night in the Greenhorn [Wet] Mountains, in 1873, when she slept out away from her companions, and where, after several months of unceasing labor, that one night broke her down and made her lip hang down as it never hung before and never did again. Soon, however, we came again upon the tracks of the train, and her long ears pricked up and she became so excited over it that I could scarcely keep her in a walk. When the camp-fire appeared and she got the scent of her companions, she seemed perfectly happy and contented, as we were also. For some distance below camp the stream-bed had widened out into quite a little valley, which continued above camp up to the head of the stream.

The next day, August 22, we made the ascent of the Rio Grande Pyramid. The day was beautiful to its close, a remarkable circumstance for this season of the year in these mountains. As we were camped at the foot of the mountain, we had plenty of time. Wishing to give the mules a little rest, Mr. Wilson directed Ford, one of the packers, to follow after and bring them back to camp. We rode up the west slope of the mountain to near 13,000 feet elevation. Taking off our instruments, we threw the stirrups over the saddles, and fixed the bridles and ropes so that they could not get caught in the timber. We then tried to start the mules back to camp by throwing stones at them. They would move off a little, but if we tried to drive them farther they would dodge back. The reason seemed to be that they had noticed that camp always was made in a different place each day, and they were afraid of getting lost if they strayed off. Their great horror of getting lost was very noticeable in many cases. In every case where we had to hunt for the camp after dark, they seemed to give

Rio Grande Pyramid, showing the west ridge which Rhoda's party used to gain the summit—*Mike Foster, 1982.*

up entirely and put their whole trust in their riders. Often have we left them loose, at elevations ranging from 12,000 to 13,000 feet, far above the timber-line, but they never attempted to stray away, although they would crop whatever grass they could find near. At times when they could not be tied so as to get enough grass, we would take off saddle and bridle, and leave them perfectly loose, but it seemed to make no difference.

The climb on foot was quite easy, and was not more than about 1,000 feet vertical. On the top we found a nicely-built monument of stones, which we increased in height to about 6 feet. Some enterprising climber seems to have taken a just pride in leaving his mark on this beautiful peak. The fact that the monument was on the true summit indicated the fact that its builder was something else than a common miner.[61] The height of this peak (station 21) is 13,773 feet above the sea.

The view from here is very fine. The whole mass of the quartzite peaks, so often mentioned as prominent features in the views from previous stations, from here stand out clearer than from any point yet visited. Almost all of the higher points are clearly visible, but they are massed together in such a way that from this point the drainage of the system cannot be made out at all. In one place, to the south of us, we could see low rolling country, indicating that we were near the southern termination of the high mountains. To the east the view was very extensive, many points of the Sangre de Cristo range, east of San Luis Valley, being clearly visible at a distance of one hundred and ten miles.[62] In the descent nothing of special interest transpired.

The next day [August 23] camp was moved up near the timber-line, at the head of the creek [Middle Ute Creek], while the three of us followed up a branch coming in on the east side, and, crossing the national divide, made station 22, on the southern point of a granite ridge, at an elevation of about 13,000 feet. The divide here is very near the boundary between the trachyte and quartzite. This line marks a sudden and decided change in the nature of the topography. Station 22 is on granite, the first we had yet come across in the district, but it only appears here in a small area.

Before leaving we were again visited by an electric hail and rain storm, which soon cut short all work. Although surrounded by high peaks, rising several hundred feet above us, the phenomena seemed quite as marked as at any previous time. The whole mass of peaks west of us was soon veiled in clouds. Just as we were leaving the little knob on the end of the ridge which had formed our station, we all felt a heavy shock as if from an electric battery. Being unaccompanied by thunder, we concluded that we had been subjected to a miniature stroke of lightning. This is the last station where we felt any electricity, although we were often caught on the peaks in rain and hail storms. The next day we had a storm almost exactly similar to this one, only it was entirely unaccompanied by electricity. The date of this station (station 22) was August 23. The rain continued falling during our ride to camp, which we found located in a clump of pines, at the junction of two small streams. Like all the trees near the timber-line, these had few branches, and furnished us little protection from storms.

Next morning [August 24] the sky was pretty clear, so, without moving camp, we crossed the divide south of us,* and ascended the high quartzite mountain east of the Vallecito. This quartzite rock is very hard, and breaks off in angular fragments with almost polished faces. Where *débris*-slides are formed of these fragments it is found that the rocks slip and slide on each other very easily. Sometimes we would step on a stone weighing several tons; it would tip up, as if delicately balanced, or slip from under us. These seem to be universal characteristics of quartzite *débris*, so that in climbing over it great care is required. This peak was very steep and difficult to climb; in fact, more so than any which we had yet ascended.

When we had nearly reached the summit, and at an elevation of 13,600 feet, a small grizzly bear suddenly jumped up a few yards in front of us and rushed down the steep slide on the south face of the peak. Of course, in a climb as long and difficult as this, our instruments and books were all we cared about bringing with us, and for this reason our guns were left behind. We were much surprised to see an animal in this

---

*Hinsdale 2 to La Plata 1.

♦

place. It is ever thus; when you feel you are treading a path never trod by a living thing before, and your imagination begins to build for itself a romantic picture, if some such vile, worldly thing as a paper collar or a whisky-bottle does not intrude itself on the sight, some beastly quadruped needs must break the precious solitude and scatter your airy castle to the winds. To show our utter disgust for all animate things that could not live below this altitude, we yelled and threw stones after the bear till he finally was lost to sight far down the mountain-side. In our hate we even wished he might have been in a position whence we could have rolled rocks down on him. As we passed on we saw several places where he or others of his breed had scraped out beds among the finer *débris*. They seemed to have come up here for fresh air, or to sun themselves, or both. After this experience we named the peak Mount Oso, from the Spanish word for bear.

As we neared the top of the peak the clouds coming from the west began to touch the summit, and we expected that the electricity would prevent any work. As we came up into the cloud we felt no electricity, at which we were much surprised. Setting up the instrument, we worked for about an hour, getting sights through the clouds, for as yet the storm had not fully commenced. The height of this point is 13,640 feet.

A number of sharp, distinct peaks, all quartzite, rise up in this vicinity from 2,000 to 4,000 feet above their bases, and all are very steep and rugged, more like needles than mountains. A number of little lakes are dotted here and there at the heads of the cañons. To the west, across the Vallecito, the view into the high quartzites was much obstructed by clouds. To the northwest, at a distance of about six miles, in the center of the group, was a high peak of vertical strata, and all the upper portion formed of great vertical pillars of quartzite. It seemed to be on the center of upheaval, as on the two sides of it the strata inclined in different directions. Its elevation is about 13,783 feet.[63]

In the immediate vicinity of our station the strata dipped at every possible angle, and appeared so complicated that only a very detailed study could ever bring order out of the chaos.

In our descent from the peak we got pretty thoroughly

drenched, and found our mules looking disconsolate. We had left them near the second little lake northeast of Mount Oso.*

Crossing the pass near this lake,** we passed over to our camp on Rio Grande waters, encountering much miry ground on the way. The rain continued falling steadily all day and all night. The next morning the creek near our camp was flooded, as were also our little tents. Rain continued next morning, and as the elevation of this camp was 11,600 feet, and the timber thin and scattering, it was a poor place to remain during a storm. We remained in camp all day [August 25]. By standing in the rain before the log fire we succeeded in drying ourselves nearly as fast as we got wet.

Hoping that it would clear off, we did not start early the next morning, but seeing no prospect of a change in the weather, we saddled up early in the forenoon and departed for other scenes. Our supply of provisions was getting very short, and we could not remain longer. All our flour had already given out, while the dried apples, beans, and even the bacon were beginning to draw to their close. With all these solemn facts staring us in the face, the caravan started about 10 o'clock a.m. [August 26]. Our course lay up the creek and over the pass[+] we had crossed the day previous.[64] We found the whole country flooded. Naturally very boggy, the ground was now so full of water that it almost floated.

The next morning [August 27] the rain still continued. As the supplies were getting short so fast, we concluded to strike the nearest way for Howardville. Moreover, we were getting disgusted with this part of the country, and wanted to find a better camping-ground. Accordingly, we moved up the main branch of the Vallecito. It was running considerable risk, as without a trail to guide us we felt doubtful about being able to cross the [continental] divide. The rain fell fast, and we were soon soaked to the skin. The grade being very steep, we rose in elevation very fast, and soon found snow and rain falling together, and we nearly froze. We stopped at one place

---

*Vicinity of Rock Lake.

**La Plata 1 to Hinsdale 2.

[+]Hinsdale 2 to San Juan.

and made a fire by which to warm our feet, but the wood was so soaked with water that we found it a difficult task. The train was behind and did not catch up; so Wilson and I heaped all the logs that were lying handy upon the fire, and, as we found later, the rest of the party made good use of the fire.

Near the head of the creek the slope became very steep and rose up to the divide, which, at the point at which we crossed it, was nearly 13,000 feet in elevation. A keen, strong breeze did not serve to add to our comfort in our present saturated condition. While waiting here for the train, Mr. Wilson made station 24 on a point east of that where we crossed the ridge. The elevation of this place is about 12,700 feet—a little higher than the point where we crossed the same divide a few days ago.

We traveled down that branch of the Rio Grande which heads between stations 24 and 25, and camped in a splendid grove of pines.* In the afternoon the sky had begun to lighten up. Isolated clouds passed swiftly over us from the west, ever and anon cutting off the sunlight, and producing the sudden chilling effect always noticeable in the shadow of a cloud at high altitudes. The great difference of temperature in the sun and in the shade at these altitudes is very remarkable. At this particular time I thought I noticed that whirls and gusts of wind always accompanied the fast-moving shadow. Whenever a long space between clouds allowed the sun to shine un-obstructed, for some time the air would be quite still, but the next cloud-shadow seemed to bring with it little whirlwinds and changing gusts of chilly air. By the time we had unsaddled our animals the sun was shining brightly, and now, after four days and three nights of incessant rain, we had a good oppor-tunity to dry our clothes and blankets, and every one made good use of the short time before sunset.

In the evening, instead of sitting down to a hearty meal, we had to make our supper on bacon and dried apples alone, and very short rations at that. We had a few beans left, but all the bacon and apples were used up for supper; but as we expected

---

*Bear Creek, below Kite Lake.

Scene Near Station 24: The Guardian (left), Mount Silex and Vallecito Lake— *Mike Foster, 1982.*

to reach Howardville the next day, we did not mind it very much.

Our bill of fare next morning [August 28] presented only two articles—beans, which on account of our elevation could not be well cooked, and sugar. We could take either or both as we chose. Beans with other food are very strengthening, but alone we could scarcely eat them at all.

The pack-train started direct to Howardville, while Wilson and I climbed the most northern of the quartzite peaks, a point having an elevation of 13,576 feet above the sea.* The day was clear, still, and beautiful. After riding as far as we could, we still had about a thousand feet to climb on foot over the steep *débris*-slides before reaching the top. We soon discovered that our breakfast of beans and sugar formed a poor foundation for such hard work. Once on top, a row of ten distinct peaks stretched in a nearly east and west line before our eyes. Their ruggedness may be understood from the illustration of "the Quartzite Peaks from station 38," the three or four on the left of the picture being just in front of us from station 25. Being much nearer, they appeared much more rugged than from station 38. The peaks in this row range from 13,560 to 13,831 feet in elevation. Between them we could see the higher peaks to the south.

The great and essential differences in the topography resulting from the change in the geological formation is here so very marked and is so interesting that I cannot pass it by without notice. The general difference in the appearance of the country in trachyte and quartzite formations is intended to be shown by the two large topographical sketches presented in this report. The view of Mount Sneffels from station 29 [Fig. 11] shows nothing but trachyte rock, while the sketch from station 38 [Fig. 15]shows quartzite only. But a mere sketch cannot show well the characteristics of the two. I have tried to work out some of the features peculiar to the topography of each of these two formations. These being derived almost wholly from observations in Southern Colorado and for the great part

---

*White Dome, or station 25.

in this particular region, they may not have a very general application.

First, then, in trachyte or volcanic rocks, the lava-flows being for the most part horizontal, the rock fractures vertically, and the falling away of pieces produces bluffs which are generally very nearly vertical. Moreover, from the nature of the flow, horizontal lines or bands are left running across the faces of all the bluffs. This latter is very characteristic of the formation.

Second. At the bases of the bluffs *débris*-slopes commence, and sweep down generally in graceful curves to a greater or less distance.

Third. These slopes are seldom very steep for any great distance, the great fall from the mountain-summits to the valleys being by way of high bluffs and comparatively gentle *débris*-slopes. In other words, the total fall is very irregularly distributed over the distance from the top to the base of the mountain.

Fourth. The junction-line of the bluffs and *débris*-slopes is almost always distinctly marked.

On the other hand, in quartzite formations—

First. Bluffs vertical, or nearly so, are very common; except in very rare cases there are no marked horizontal lines.

Second. The junction between the bluffs and *débris*-slopes is never so distinctly marked as in trachyte.

Third. On account of the fact that this rock breaks off in large angular fragments, and also on account of its great hardness, it will lie at a much steeper slope than the other rock. From the same causes the loose rock does not take on those beautiful sweeping curves so common in volcanic rocks, but have a certain stiffness of line.

Fourth. The solid rock, from its great hardness and the manner of its crystallization, is often found in very steep, yet quite irregular slopes, without taking on the form of bluff. A noticeable instance of this is the most easterly of the ten peaks mentioned above.* The fall from its summit to Vallecito Creek on the east is 3,000 feet in less than a mile horizontal, or a mean slope of nearly 32°; yet it is a plain slope of solid rock,

---

*The Guardian, 13,617 feet.

more or less irregular, of course, but having no bluff in all that distance. On the north side of the same peak there is a slope at an angle of 60° to 80° for not less than 2,000 feet, yet there is no part of it bluff.

Still another point is the fact that in the metamorphism of the original sedimentary rocks into quartzite, the great natural convulsions attending that process have distorted the strata terribly, so that, as in this particular region, a number of peaks in a small area may each have its strata dipping at a different angle from all the rest. The effect of this on topography may be seen in the sketch from station 38. The high peak next to the last one on the left shows in a marked manner that the strata incline to the right, or southward. The high peak near the middle of the sketch, being in the center of upheaval, has vertical strata, while those farther to the right incline to the north. This latter fact is not so well shown in this sketch, but from some other points of view it appears very plainly. These facts show how the form of the peaks may differ in the same kind of rocks; but as there is little or none of this upsetting of the lava-flows, there must result a distinct type of mountain-form for each. The peculiar crystallization of the quartzite has also a marked effect on the forms.

In accordance with these facts, we find that quartzite mountains are generally much more rugged, but lacking the relief given to those in volcanic regions by the contrast of the bluffs with the *débris*-slopes. The boundary of the quartzite on the north follows closely the national divide.[65]

On our return to Howardville [still August 28] we rode across the rolling ground which extends southward from Cunningham Pass. Arriving at the town, we found Mr. Jackson, the photographer of the expedition, with his party. He had just arrived from the Los Pinos agency. We made the ascent of Sultan Mountain* with him, and he succeeded in getting a number of good photographs of the surrounding country. From this point is obtained by far the best view of Baker's Park that is obtainable from any peak in the vicinity.[66]

After getting our supplies we marched up Mineral Creek

---

*Station 26.

The "Quartzites" (background) and Grand Turk (center) from the top of Sultan Mountain—*Courtesy USGS, W.H. Jackson, 1874.*

[September 2], while Mr. Jackson struck south over the trail which passes around the west side of Sultan Mountain, and made a very interesting investigation of the old ruins in Southwestern Colorado.

In the afternoon rain fell, and continued into the night, but th next morning was cold and the sky clear and beautiful. This date (September 3) is remarkable as being the time of the abrupt change between summer and fall. After this, till the snow-storms commenced, the weather was cold and clear.

Having camped overnight at the junction of Bear [South Fork] and Mineral Creeks, the next morning [still September 3], we moved up the latter, and made stations 27* and 28** on a high ridge between Mineral and Cement Creeks.

Camping near the head of the creek, the following day [September 4] we crossed the pass[†] at its head and passed over to the head of the Uncompahgre River.[67] The elevation of this pass is 11,100 feet above the sea. It is entirely covered with timber. The slope to the south is quite gradual, but to the north, down the Uncompahgre, the fall is 800 feet in two miles. Then for several miles the stream flows comparatively smoothly, till it finally enters a deep box-cañon, where the fall is very great. Traveling for some distance is both difficult and dangerous. At the bottom of the first steep slope a great area of fallen timber commences. The logs so cover the ground that traveling is very nearly impossible.

Leaving a notice for the pack-train to camp near the beginning of this dead timber, Mr. Wilson, Dr. Endlich, and I rode on, and finally got through the timber, when we had open grassy ground to travel over, but the slope was so steep that we could ride only a small part of the way. Leaving our mules loose, as usual, to find what grass they might at this elevation, which was a little less than 13,000 feet, we made station 29, on a round-topped peak, which, being surrounded by peaks higher than itself, is of no great importance. It was taken as a station, because its position between two of the main

---

*Ohio Peak.

**Red Mountain No. 3.

[†]San Juan to Ouray 2.

branches of the Uncompahgre made it a key-point for the drainage system which forms the head of that stream. Its elevation is 13,206 feet.

From this point we got by far the best view of Mount Sneffels, and the curious pinnacle-forms in its vicinity, which have already been mentioned as seen from station 10. The accompanying illustration, taken from a hasty topographical sketch, will give a faint idea of the great peak and its vicinity. Of course the elevation and ruggedness of the mountains shown in the sketch can only be appreciated by a person who has climbed many mountains. Even then the air is so clear at these high altitudes that one is deceived in spite of himself with regard to distances. From here we could see no feasible route by which to climb the great Mount Sneffels, so we laid the question aside till a view from some peak farther to the west should solve it satisfactorily.

Next day [September 5] we retraced our steps over the pass* and down Mineral Creek, camping again at its junction with Bear Creek [South Fork].

Moving up the latter stream, we camped [still September 5] on a considerable branch which comes in from the north.** This is probably the finest camping-ground on the whole stream, with fine timber, good water, and a sufficient quantity of grass. Above this there is a dense grove of timber, through which you pass up a pretty steep slope; in a short distance the pines end, and you come out into an open space, extending several miles up the stream, and covered with a remarkably rich growth of weeds and shrubs. This circumstance is probably explained by the fact that here a great part of the lower slopes of the cañon is composed of red sandstone, which seems to produce a much better soil than the volcanic rock.

The next day (September 6) we made the ascent of the highest peak in this vicinity.† It is marked station 30 on the map, and has an elevation of 13,897 feet. The climb was difficult, on account of the long slopes of loose *débris* up which

---

*Ouray 2 to San Juan.

**Probably Clear Creek.

†Vermillion Peak.

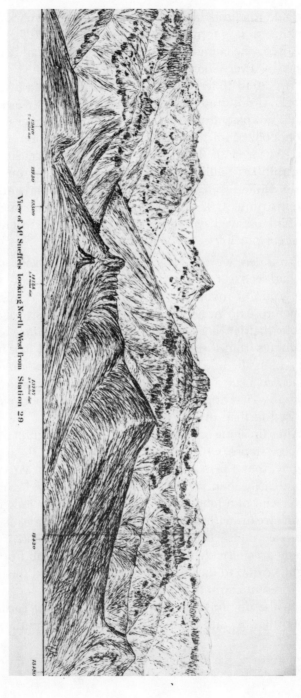

View of Mt Sneffels looking North West from Station 29.

Mt. Sneffels From Station 29. Teakettle Mountain is the high point (13,819')
just to the right of Mt. Sneffels in this sketch by Rhoda from the first printing
(1875) of his *Report—Mel Ryan-Roberts, 1983.*

63

we had to climb. The top of the peak was remarkable for its smallness. it is formed of two knobs, about 20 feet apart, the northern one being a little the higher, and connected with the other by a very sharp ridge. To the west was a slope of 60° or 70° for 30 to 40 feet, then a precipice of about a thousand feet nearly, if not quite, vertical. When the tripod was set up, we could not pass around it, but had to crawl under it. We three monopolized all the sitting and standing room on the peak. Mr. Wilson with the instrument completely covered the true summit. Dr. Endlich took his geological notes from the lower knob, while I sketched, sitting at the edge of and almost under the instrument. The slopes, on all sides but the narrow path we had followed, were very steep, and in a few feet terminated in great precipices.

From here we got a splendid view of Mount Wilson, which we had seen from many stations before this, but always across the group of mountains of which station 30 formed a part. Now it rose up grandly, forming the most massive of any peaks in our district, and, judging from its appearance and rough estimates from the angles of elevation, we felt that it must be very high. In line with the peak, but several miles nearer, appeared Lizard's [Lizard] Head, a peculiar pinnacle, which from this view appears quite broad. It will be more particularly noticed farther on.

After finishing our observations, we built a small monument of loose stones, which, when finished, covered the top so completely, that a person could not pass around it. We descended more easily than we had ascended, and found camp at the lower end of a long patch of timber, near the junction of the main stream with the last tributary which comes in from the south as you travel up.* This marks the upper end of the open, weedy area already mentioned. The total climb from our last night's camp to the station was 4,000 feet, and the descent to our present camp 3,200 feet.

On the day following [September 7] we let camp remain where it was, and rode up the creek to the south of us, and

---

*Vicinity of Bandora Mine.

over the divide,* to Engineer Mountain. On the way we had to pass around a peculiar amphitheater, which had been eroded out of the red sandstone. The stratification of the sandstone had produced benches, which extended all the way around the head of a little stream which flows into Cascade Creek. We found the ascent of the peak not very tiresome, but rather dangerous. We climbed up the ridge from the east. On our right was the great bluff, which is nearly a thousand feet in height and almost vertical. On the southeast side the rock weathered off in small plate-like fragments, producing innumerable cracks and little shelves, but none large enough to give a secure foot-hold. The slope on this side is very steep, so that if a person should slip he could not possibly save himself from destruction. Mr. Prout in 1873 ascended this same peak from the south side, which I should judge is much the safer, but at the same time the longer and more tiresome way. From this point we had a splendid view down the Animas. Animas Park was visible, and the low country in its vicinity showed us that the high mountains were nearly at an end. A group of pretty high peaks were to be seen to the southwest, called the La Plata Mountains. They are completely isolated from the main mass of the range by many miles of comparatively low land. On our return to camp a sudden and heavy shower of rain came up, but cleared off soon after.

The next day [September 8] found us on our way through the patch of timber already mentioned. The trail passes through the center of the group, which is very swampy, and our animals mired many times before we got through. We found relief only at the timber-line, after which we rode on, over grass and fine rock-slopes, up to the pass,** which has an elevation, according to our aneroid barometers, of 12,600 feet.[68] It is certainly the highest of all the passes leading out of Baker's Park.

A pass which I think will be found much better, crosses the range about six miles to the northeast of this.† To go this way

---

*Just north of Jura Knob.
**San Juan to San Miguel 3.
†Ophir Pass.

you must travel up the largest tributary of Mineral Creek,*
which comes in from the west, and cross over on to a tributary
of the San Miguel. This pass is not less than a thousand feet
lower, and, at least to the west, has a much better grade.

Passing over from Bear Creek [South Fork] to the head of
the San Miguel [Lake Fork], after a sudden descent of several
hundred feet, we came to a small lake.** Further down, the
slope was more gradual for some distance, till we came to a
steep *débris*-slide, down which the trail led to the valley below.
The fall from the pass to the valley, by way of the trail, is
2,800 feet in two miles. On the east side of the pass the rise
from the stream-junction, where we [had] camped, to the
pass is 2,000 feet in two miles.

Station 30 rose up boldly just to the north of us as we rode
down the trail. Its side was worn out into beautiful forms,
and the delicate blending of the full red and yellow colors of
the rocks, taken together with the long sweeps of the *débris*-
slides, gave this peak a finer appearance than any we had yet
seen.[69] Once down in the little valley below, we found trees
and grass growing very luxuriantly. The trail crosses several
boggy places, over which our mules passed with difficulty.

A few miles down stream from the head of the little valley
is San Miguel [Trout] Lake, a very beautiful sheet of water,
filled with fine trout. We stopped to make a compass station
on the edge of the lake, and took a reading with the mercurial
barometer, which makes the elevation 9,720 feet. Thence we
traveled down the San Miguel River [Lake Fork, then South
Fork], along a very old, disused Indian trail; in some places,
considerable trees lying across it showed that it had not been
used for many years. For some distance below the lake, the
San Miguel [South Fork], which is here a pretty large creek,
flows quite gently; but further down the slope suddenly in-
creases, and the stream is broken up into falls and cascades.
In going down the trail, at this point, we found the slope so
steep that we had to dismount and lead our mules, till we
reached the bed of a large creek which comes into the San

---

*That would be Middle Fork.
**Lake Hope.

66

Trout Lake Panorama. Bear Creek Pass is the depression just right of center. Station 30 (Vermillion Peak) rises above the ridge to the left of the Pass— *Courtesy USGS, W.H. Jackson, 1874.*

Miguel [South Fork] from the east.* After crossing this the trail ascends the north slope of the cañon, which is quite steep. The total fall, from the lake down to the junction of this creek with the main stream, is about 900 or 1,000 feet in a distance of two and a half miles. At least 600 feet of this fall takes place in the last mile. At the bottom is a fine fall, which from a distance we judged to be not less than a hundred feet in height.

After crossing the cañon of the creek above mentioned we came out on a pretty smooth area, covered with scattering timber and fine grass. One thing very peculiar about this particular part of the country is the deathlike stillness that almost oppresses one in passing through it. There is the finest growth of grass I have ever seen in Colorado, with beautiful little groves of pine and quaking asp scattered about, which one would expect to be full of game. The old trail and the very antiquated appearance of the carvings on the trees, and the absence of all tracks, old or new, indicated that the Indians had abandoned this route long since. With all these conditions, so favorable to animal life, we did not hear a bird twitter in the thickets, and saw neither deer, elk, nor antelope, nor even a single track of one of those animals. In all other parts of the country little squirrels and chipmunks were seen in abundance; but here, if they existed at all, they kept themselves close. We made camp on the large east fork** of the San Miguel, just across the stream from station 32 on the map.

The next day, September 9, we made station 32, on a low hill on the north side of the creek, which from its width might more properly be called a river. Above this for several miles the stream-bed is very flat and covered with willows, while the stream itself winds like a great snake. A short distance below our station the stream plunges down very abruptly into the cañon of the San Miguel, which, above and below this junction, cuts down from 800 to 1,000 feet into the sandstone which here makes its appearance.

Leaving station 32 on our way to Mount Sneffels, we followed

---

*Howard Fork.

**Now the San Miguel itself.

the trail a short distance, and then, turning off to the right, with great difficulty succeeded in descending to the bed of a creek flowing from the northeast.[70] In this vicinity we saw a band of six gray wolves, the first we had seen during the season.

With great difficulty we followed up the canyon, which gradually became narrower and more rocky. In some places we had to cross over short spaces of smooth, almost polished rock-surfaces, inclined toward the stream. In one such place a small rivulet of water flowed over the surface and terminated below in a fall of considerable height. The smooth stone, thus wet, rendered our passage with the mule-train very hazardous, as the least slip would have resulted in the certain destruction of an animal, and possibly serious injury to members of the party. As we traveled upward the trees became more and more scattering, and the huge rock-slides, which below we had only seen high up against the mountain-sides, began to extend their fingers, like glaciers, far below the timber-line, and in many places reached the bed of the creek. These slides, ever and anon crossing our path, rendered travel very difficult for animals; the more so as they were composed of large angular fragments, often many tons in weight, and containing in their interstices no vestige of soil or vegetation. Sometimes we were able, by filling in the spaces with small stones, to form a rough trail over these. At others, we were able to go around them.

The obstacles to our onward march continued to grow greater and greater till we came to the upper verge of a clump of trees, and found our further progress completely barred by the great *débris*-slides on both sides of the creek, coming down to the water's edge, making the passage for animals an utter impossibility. About half a mile farther on we could see the trees commence again; but this strait, if we may call it such, was too much for us. Besides, we could see no prospect of good grass for the animals ahead, while this last group of trees formed a beautiful camping ground, and was overgrown with a rich crop of grass. There, then, we made camp; and as it was early in the afternoon, and the sun shining brightly, we took this rare opportunity of spreading out our blankets to dry.

Wilson turned out his mule with the rest to feed, and walked on over the rock-slides, up the cañon, to reconnoiter, and after a long and tiresome walk reached the summit of the pass at the head of the gulch,[71] and saw, far across, a curious sink-like amphitheater, the object of our journey, looming up in terrible blackness before him.* He saw at a glance that from our present position the peak must be ascended in one day, from our present camp, all on foot. The mountain had to be climbed, and the only easier ascent was from the north. But to get to that side of the mountain necessitated a circuitous journey of several days around the portion of the mountains jutting out to the west.

On his return to camp in the evening he reported the result of his deliberations to the rest of the party, and it was concluded to make the ascent from our present camp. We all knew well that the winter-storms would soon commence, and we could ill afford to lose the time necessary to go around to the north side of the mountain. The present camp is marked on the map as camp 45.

ASCENT OF MOUNT SNEFFELS[72]

The next morning [September 10] we provided ourselves with lunches, as was our custom, and the three of us set out on foot at six o'clock, with our note-books and instruments. The first portion of the climb to the pass above mentioned, was in a northeasterly direction from camp. After crossing the portion of *débris* already described we came again to timber, then to soil covered with very short grass but devoid of other vegetation. After leaving the timber we could see about us, and a dreary sight we saw. Near us was nothing but these great angular fragments of trachytic rock, which, in the distance, faded to a dull, dreary, gray tint. In some places these slides formed long, regular, slightly curved lines; in others the stone appeared in swells like sand-dunes.

The head of the cañon was amphitheatrical in form, like almost all in lava regions. On the east side we noticed particularly a sub-amphitheater, which, being composed of nothing but the loose *débris*, variegated by neither shrub nor blade of grass nor even barren soil, nor by any change of color in the

---

*The valley of Blue Lakes.

70

rock, presented one of the most desolate sights that meets the eye of the mountain-climber. The weird stillness of high altitudes, only served to heighten the appearance of desolation about us, and gave one the idea that all nature was dead.

Passing from the small area of soil over which we traveled after leaving the timber, we came again to the loose *débris*. Take note of that little patch of soil, for we may not step on soil again till we return at night from our tiresome climb. We now had to walk over the loose bowlders, stepping from stone to stone. This was very tiresome, as we could not relax our attention for a single moment for fear we should step on a balanced stone, and fall or slip on some smooth surface. Toward the last, the ascent became very steep, and we had to climb with great care. The last few hundred feet was just about as steep as loose rock would lie. We thought nothing of this, however, as we were fresh, and knew, besides, that this was the easiest part of our day's journey.

We reached the pass at last, and as we had been climbing till then in the shadow we were glad to see the sun rising clear and beautiful.* Everything seemed to conspire to make a beautiful day, and we lacked only time to let our imaginations run on and make a sublimely-romantic picture of sunrise at a high elevation. The claw-marks on the rocks, on either side of the summit of the pass, showed that the grizzly had been before us. We gave up all hope of ever beating the bear climbing mountains. Several times before, when, after terribly difficult and dangerous climbs, we had secretly chuckled over our having outwitted Bruin at last, some of the tribe had suddenly jumped up not far from us and taken to their heels over the loose rocks. Mountain-sheep we had beaten in fair competition, but the bear was "one too many for us."

After stopping a few moments to draw our breath, we had a little leisure to look around us. Looking back we could see the clump of trees, 3,000 feet below us, in which camp was situated; while in front of us, and behind us, and around us, appeared nothing but miles and miles of loose rock, with rocky peaks everywhere.

---

*San Miguel 3 to Ouray 2.

Immediately in front of us was a curious depression, which, at its lowest point, was about 2,000 feet below us, although we were standing on the lowest point of the ridge surrounding it. It covered several square miles in area; it seemed to be completely closed up, as no outlet could be seen. It was apparently walled in on all sides.

On our right a bluff ran clear around to the great mountain, and was very nearly vertical for full a thousand feet, at some points more. For three miles from this pass, along the ridge on the south side of the amphitheater, no point is less than 13,500 feet in elevation, while several peaks rise above 13,700, and one above 13,800 feet.* Just to the south of Mount Sneffels was another comparatively low gap, which we felt was passable for good foot-climbers.** This and the pass on which we stood were the only visible outlets; excepting these two, which were only just passable to men on foot, we could see no break in the great Chinese wall around this little empire of desolation and death-like stillness.

We knew, of course, that there must be an outlet, and we knew where that outlet must be, but we saw none; we knew that the wall around the south side from us to the great peak, was continuous, and we could see that there was no break in the north wall for a considerable distance. The only point we were not sure of was at the northeast corner of the basin, just west of the peak. We were certain the outlet must be there, merely because we knew it could be nowhere else; however interesting it might have been from a geological point of view, it made our hearts sink within us to look at it. In making the ascent of a mountain, there is nothing more painful than to find a deep gorge or sink crossing your path; you know that all the distance you go down must be climbed up again before you reach once more your present level.

We did not remain on the pass long enough to think half that I have written, for it has always been a maxim with us that every minute saved in the morning brings us back to camp so much earlier in the evening, and we can never tell

---

*Dallas Peak, 13,809 feet.

**Blue Lakes Pass.

how long a climb is going to take us. We find sufficient time while climbing to observe the scenery around us in a very general way, but the romance of our work is not fully appreciated by us till we reach civilization, where we can find leisure to think over what we have seen; at the time no romance is visible.

Almost due east of us and across the sink, at a distance of three miles, was Mount Sneffels, the end and aim of our labors. We traveled over the sunken area a considerable time, as it is several miles across. As we went on, it became more and more evident that the "fallen-in" appearance of this depressed area was not mere appearance. Evidence presented itself on all sides to prove that this great area had actually sunk in one mass several hundred feet. After a time the descent became much steeper, and we were much surprised on looking back to see behind us a peak rising up to a considerable height. The truth was, that it was only a ridge the same height as the main part of the amphitheater, and only presented the appearance of a peak from below. Near this point we were joined by Ford, one of the packers, who had concluded that he wanted to climb a peak, too, and had chosen this one, the hardest climb of the season. The lowest point of the amphitheater was the head of a cañon leading out to the north. In the bottom of this was a small lake with an elevation of nearly 12,000 feet.*

It was rather a pleasure than otherwise when we began to ascend again. Now we were sure that we had no more gorges or sinks to cross, but that, excepting the ups and downs common to all peaks, our way lay upward. A few hundred feet above the bottom of the sink we came upon a bench on which were two small lakes, while just beyond, the steep, rugged mountain rose up. The first half of the height was very steep, but neither so tiresome nor so dangerous as the last half. The first was a plain slope extending from the lakes to the ridge of which the peak formed the termination. After reaching this we had to follow the sharp ridge of the mountain, which for a considerable distance was notched much like a comb. The crystallization was nearly vertical, and we could not follow

---

*Lower Blue Lake, at 11,000 feet.

Mt. Sneffels From the Northwest. The sharp, notched ridge Rhoda climbed
is on the right—*Mike Foster, 1982.*

along the highest line of the ridge, but had to go down the spaces between the teeth of the comb, then climb hand over hand up the steep bluff beyond, and so on until, within a few hundred feet of the top, the rock suddenly changed and was worn into more or less rounded slopes, all considerably polished, but beveled out in a curious manner, by the weather. These slight bevels were our only foot-holds, and, as the slope was quite steep in some places, we had to climb with care; but all our labor was soon rewarded by the glorious view which presented itself to us when we reached the top.

On the west and north sides the peak was precipitous, while on the east it sloped much more gradually. It was situated on the extreme north edge of the range, and fell in very steep slopes to the low valley of the Uncompahgre, to the north. On all sides but this we were surrounded by rugged peaks and impassable cañons. The great fact which was instantly impressed upon our minds was the great area of the surface above timber-line. In fact, toward the east, south, and west, with the exception of a clump here and there, at great intervals, no timber was visible.

Leading from the southeast side of the peak was a cañon, which, for a considerable distance down, ran nearly due east, but continually veering more and more toward the north.* For several miles down, the slopes to the bed were very gentle, and presented the appearance of a deep hollow rather than that of a gorge; but it became more and more rugged toward its mouth, till finally, within a few miles of that point, it was almost impassable, till at last it joined the truly great cañon of the Uncompahgre River. This latter cañon and its vicinity is one of the most curious places in the district. The ridges running down to it both from the east and west sides are curiously notched and cut into strange shapes. Numerous high, sharp pinnacles, clustering together here and there, appear like church-steeples, while in other places the weathering of bluffs has produced the appearance of niches with statuary. We noticed several large quartz veins which seemed never to have been discovered by the miners.

---

*Sneffels Creek-Canyon Creek drainage.

Across this space, and far above it, we saw Uncompahgre Peak, which showed us the familiar precipice on the north side, with the terraced slope on the south. Though presenting to our eyes the same profile as when we were approaching it from the east, we had lost much of our awe of the mountain from the fact that we had found so many that were harder to climb. We could see distinctly every station we had been on, so far, this summer, besides many of the year previous.[73]

The group of quartzite peaks stood up as boldly as ever about thirty miles to the southeast. In fact, I may state here that we have never yet seen the group from any station (and we have viewed it from all sides) without feeling both deep respect and awe for their terrible ruggedness. The fact already stated, that the storm-clouds seem to hover about them before starting on their meandering ways, only served to add to our other feelings one of uneasiness. It may be that the vivid recollection of a long and dreary storm encountered in that region, made it appear to us in an exaggerated form.

A little nearer, and slightly to the left of them, we could plainly see and distinguish all the peaks surrounding Baker's Park and the great mining region. Still nearer, and seeming almost under us, was station 28, with its associates, in the little cluster of deep red-colored peaks along the water-shed, between Mineral Creek and the Uncompahgre.

The view directly south of us presented the greatest mass of peaks to be seen in any direction. In that direction we look longitudinally along the range of peaks which forms the west line of the great mountain-mass, from which there is a very abrupt descent to the western plateau system. Chief among these stood station 30, which we had visited only a few days before, while about nine [ten] miles to the [north]west of it was the high peak which we were soon to climb, but whose top was veiled in clouds, only the massive base and a few of the subordinate peaks being visible.* West of it were several low, sharp peaks scattered here and there, but these soon sloped off into the plain, which extended to the horizon, broken only by the deep cañons which have been cut in the red

---

*Mount Wilson, station 35.

sandstone by the streams.

Directly to the west, in the far distance, was the group of the Sierra La Sal Mountains,[74] and scattered about the horizon, south of them, we could see several very distant mountains, which were so far away that their blue color could scarcely be distinguished from that of the sky.

Immediately to the north of us, and far below us, was the valley of the Uncompahgre, which, on both sides, seemed to have quite a gradual slope toward the stream. To us, viewing it from this great elevation, it presented the appearance of being covered with a rich growth of grass, though of this fact we could not be sure from so great a distance. The junction of the Uncompahgre with the Gunnison was distinctly marked by the vegetation along the banks of the two streams. We could see the course some distance below the junction, but it soon faded into the distance, and no one could say, from what he saw, what way the water had gone.

Beyond the Gunnison, on the north, there appeared a very elevated plateau, which, commencing near the mountain-peaks, presented a nearly horizontal profile for a considerable distance, and then, slowly increasing, its slope fell off almost insensibly to the west. Still farther around to the right, and about northeast of us, we could see most of the great peaks west of the Arkansas River.[75] Many others appeared behind, but we did not trouble our minds about recognizing them, as all our time was necessary for the more immediate details of the topography around us.

The great length of time required to ascend and descend again prevented us from remaining long. We had reached the top about noon, and found that we could not possibly remain over two hours and expect to get to camp; and since there was not a stick of timber on the way we dared not sleep out, even though the work on the peak had to be cut short. Our time being up, we raised a monument of loose stones about five feet high and started for camp.

The descent to the lakes was very easy and did not require much time, but, as we expected, the climb up to the pass again began to tell on us, and a weakness in our legs showed what a terrible strain on our systems the morning's climb had been. We finally reached the pass just in time to see the sun setting.* Some may suppose that now we sat down and rested ourselves before making the last descent down to camp. But all frequenters of the high mountains are acquainted with the fact that there, darkness follows sunset very suddenly, with scarcely any twilight between. By calling to mind this fact and estimating the obstacles between us and camp, we found that with our utmost endeavors we could not hope to get into camp till long after dark. On the other hand, we knew that we could not travel any considerable distance over the *débris* after dark, so we struck for the timber with all our speed. When darkness came on we found ourselves in a mixture of vegetation and loose rock, and had to pick our way with the utmost care.

Our long-continued exertions were at last crowned with success, and we had the pleasure of sitting down to a supper which tasted to us far better than the most costly meals of civilization, served up in the most expensive hotels. We reached camp at eight o'clock in the evening, having been fourteen hours from camp, twelve of which had been occupied in steady climbing, and two in work on the summit of the peak. During those twelve hours we had climbed up 7,000 feet, and down an equal distance, beside traveling a horizontal distance of six miles, the whole over loose rock.

The next day, which was September 11, we retraced our steps down the creek, and turning to the right followed up the west branch of the same stream.** We made station 34, whose elevation is 12,997 feet, on a peak at the head of this creek. It is the most western of the great group of mountains of which Mount Sneffels is the highest point. From here Lizard's Head, east of Mount Wilson, stood up like a high monument on the top of a mountain-peak. From this view the width of the base bears about the same relation to the height as in the great artificial monuments. The height of the column is 290 feet,[†] and the elevation of the summit above the sea 13,160 feet. From this point it is fourteen miles distant in a straight

---

*Ouray 2 to San Miguel 3.

**Deep Creek.

[†]Closer to 350 feet.

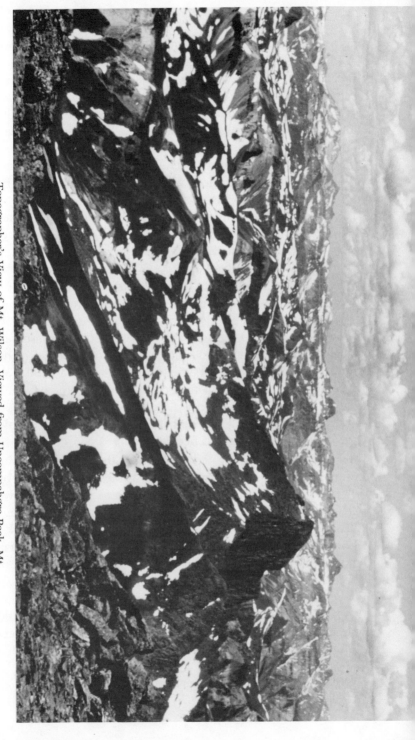

Topographer's View of Mt. Wilson. Viewed from Uncompahgre Peak, Mt. Wilson (left background) looks awesome even at a distance of some thirty-three miles. The high pyramid in the right background is Mt. Sneffels, about eighteen miles distant. The high point in the foreground is Wetterhorn Peak, 14,015'.—*Mike Foster, 1982.*

line, yet it loomed up finely. On our way to camp, which we found located at the junction of the two creeks, we saw a black bear, the first we had yet come across, but he disappeared so suddenly that it was impossible to get a shot.

We were well satisfied with having finished this part of the mountain country. Only one peak of which we had any dread remained yet to be ascended, and that was Mount Wilson.[76] From various circumstances we had reason to believe that this was higher than any station we had yet made, and from its rugged appearance we dreaded its ascent not a little.

We returned [September12] to Lake San Miguel [Trout Lake] by the same trail we had come. On our way we saw a few cranes, which, with their long legs and unearthly noises, only served to add to the funereal aspect of the scenery. At the lake Dr. Endlich and I stopped to make a detailed sketch of station 30. From here the peak, with the lake in the foreground, and the rich groups of pine and aspen, separated by spaces covered with a rank growth of grass for a middle distance, presented a beautiful appearance. Crossing over the divide between the San Miguel and Dolores,* at an elevation of about 10,200 feet, we turned off to the right and camped on a stream which flows down from the southeast side of Mount Wilson.** On the way Mr. Wilson succeeded in killing a fair-sized male grizzly with his Springfield needle-gun.

September 13 was devoted to climbing the great mountain. Riding to the timber-line, we sent our mules back to camp by one of the packers, and commenced the ascent. At first we had a low bluff of slate to get over. The plates of the stone were remarkable for their great size and freedom from cracks. Above this the climb was quite easy for a considerable distance, being nothing more than plain slopes of loose *débris*.

When we had reached an elevation of about 13,000 feet, we noticed three mountain-sheep on the top of a high ridge to the north of us, and about 1,000 feet above us. We could scarcely see how they got up there, such was the ruggedness of the ridge. They watched our progress from this elevated

---

*Lizard Head Pass. San Miguel 3 to Dolores 3.

**Slate Creek.

stand-point with great interest, now and then jumping upon a rock to get a better view. They reminded us very much of some of the illustrations in the school geographies.

A little farther on we came to a large steep snow-bank, up which we climbed with difficulty, cutting notches in the snow for foot-holds. At the upper end of this we came to what was much worse, very steep and dangerous rock-walls. From this point to the summit the stone is crystallized into vertical blocks, broken up so as to be very insecure.

Near the beginning of this part we came to a notch in the narrow ridge which was filled in by a great stone, with its upper part wedge-shaped. On the east was a fall, very nearly vertical, of two or three hundred feet, terminating below in the steep snow-bank already mentioned. On the west was a precipice many hundreds of feet in height. Over this wedge we had to pass by straddling it and sliding ourselves carefully across. The whole distance was not more than ten or fifteen feet. It seemed very much like crawling along the comb of the roof of a very high house.

Just beyond arose a steep rock-wall of loose shelving rock, up which we climbed with great difficulty, from the fact that all the rocks were loose; and even the largest could not be surely depended on.

Reaching the summit of this we had to walk for forty or fifty yards along the sharp ridge over loose blocks of stone standing on their ends. The ridge was so sharp that we had to follow the center. On either side the slopes were so nearly vertical that if a person should once slip there would be nothing to stop his descent for many hundred feet, and in some places a thousand feet or more. All the stones were so loose that we could feel them move under our feet. For a part of the distance we had to walk straight, without anything to lay our hands on. At one point in particular, we had to leap across a break in the ridge where a stone had fallen out, trusting to Providence for the firmness of the new foot-hold. This was at an elevation of nearly 14,200 feet. We came very near giving up here; but we could just get a glimpse of the main peak a little farther on, and the temptation was too strong for us.

After getting over this very dangerous part, we came to a

deep crevasse which cut across the ridge, and succeeded, with great difficulty, in getting down to the bottom of it. A thin coating of ice over many of the stones, remaining from a recent hail-storm, added greatly to the danger of the climb. Thence we had to climb around the edge of a bluff, which we found a very dangerous undertaking. Once over this we climbed out of the crevasse without difficulty and gained the longed-for summit.

We found it composed of the same rock as I have described, crystallized in vertical prisms, but crumbling away. Beyond a space probably eight or ten feet square, we could not pass without the very greatest danger of being precipitated over the terrible bluffs surrounding us on nearly all sides. We could scarcely find space enough for a monument, with room enough to pass around it. We did, however, leave a small monument of loose stones to mark this station (station 35). The thermometer stood at 33° Fahrenheit, which, with a steady breeze from the west, did not add to our comfort, especially as we had to confine our movements to such a small area. While we were up here clouds began to come from the northeast directly toward us and against the wind, apparently moved by an undercurrent, as they were below us. We could trace distinctly the track of the slight snow which fell the last night, by its marks on the peaks of the great mass.

This peak was a splendid point for a station, giving the key to the drainage and topography for miles around. To the east and north the San Miguel and its tributaries appeared to us, from our elevated stand-point, as if laid down on a map. Lizard's Head, a few miles east of us, formed a very prominent feature in the landscape, although, looking at it from our elevation (14,280 feet), its height did not show. From this direction it appears quite broad, from the fact that its greatest length is from north to south. To the west of us and quite near was a pretty high mountain.* Beyond it were scattered a number of sharp, isolated peaks, mostly under 13,000 feet in elevation, while still farther to the west extensive plateaus reached to the horizon. In the far southwest appeared several

_____
*El Diente Peak, 14,159 feet.

very dim, bluish mountains, probably considerably over a hundred miles distant. Somewhat nearer to us, and a little farther around toward the south, appeared Ute Peak, near the southwest corner of Colorado. In the far northwest the Sierra La Sal Mountains were distinctly visible. Much was also seen that has been already described as having been seen from other stations. Mount Wilson is the highest mountain in Southwestern Colorado, and by far the most massive.

The descent was made with great care, and, luckily, without accident either to ourselves or the instruments. The descent over the snow-bank was much easier than the ascent, being accomplished by simply sitting down on the snow and letting gravity do the rest. Below it, we found several holes among the loose rocks, which bears had pawed out for beds, but we met none of the animals themselves. We reached camp quite early. The total height climbed on foot was 2,500 feet. It was not very tiresome, but by far the most dangerous of all the climbs of the summer.

After this we marched a short distance down the Dolores and made stations 36 and 37.[77] After that, returning* by way of San Miguel [Trout] Lake, we recrossed the Bear Creek [South Fork] Pass,** and camped at the creek junction, where we had camped a week previous. The day after, we rode to Howardville. We had scarcely got our dinner, when Mr. Jackson and party came up from their trip to the ruins, of which they gave glowing accounts.[78]

On September 19 we started down the Animas, crossing, over the southeast slope of Sultan Mountain, by the trail. We found the trail very bad. At one point a tree-stump stood in it. Some miners passing over this route a few days before had one of their animals killed by its falling down the side of the mountain at this point. The divide is about 10,460 feet in elevation, but the highest point of the trail is several hundred feet higher.

We camped near this latter point, and the next day left the train to follow the trail a few miles and camp, while we rode

---

*Dolores 3 to San Miguel 3.

**San Miguel 3 to San Juan.

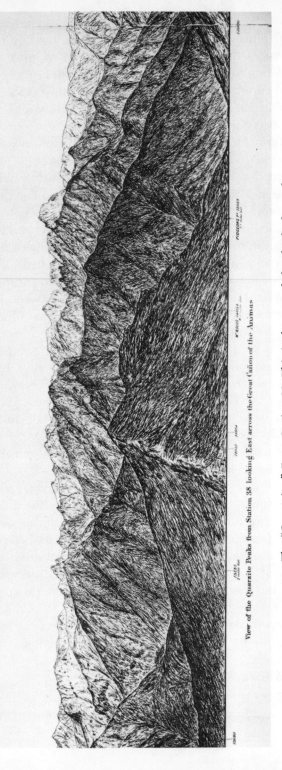

View of the Quartzite Peaks from Station 38 looking East across the Great Cañon of the Animas

The "Quartzites" From Station 38. This is the second sketch Rhoda made to accompany his *Report*—*Mel Ryan-Roberts, 1983.*

in a southeasterly direction and made station 38, on a rounded peak of quartzite, 13,046 feet in elevation.[79] From here we obtained the most striking view of the quartzite mountains. The illustration is reproduced from a topographical sketch made at this station. The point is on the brink of the great Animas Cañon, which here is over 4,000 feet in depth; a few miles farther down it is still deeper. The total length of the Grand Cañon, from the mouth of Mineral Creek down to that of Cascade, is about seventeen miles; below this, for about seven miles, it becomes very narrow and straight, with a depth of about 1,000 feet.

In returning to the trail we found the country terribly cut up along the head branches of Lime Creek, and even after reaching the trail it was not the easiest we had yet had. Judging from what I have heard and seen of the pass to the west of Sultan Mountain, I think it a much better route. Some fallen timber and swamp are encountered, but not more than on this trail. We did not travel over it ourselves; but Mr. Jackson, who has been over both, gives the trail over the western pass the preference. If ever a wagon-road can be built over into Baker's Park, from the south, it will be only by that way. The ground is very rough along the trail to a mile or so south of the crossing of Cascade Creek, when it becomes more even, and the traveling from there on is very good.* Wagons could be brought this far, from the south, without the least trouble.

A long line of sandstone bluffs extends parallel to the trail for several miles, and rise from 1,500 to 1,800 feet above it.** The trail passes along a sort of table, with these bluffs rising above it on the west side, and the Animas Cañon bounding it on the east.+

Arriving at Animas City,[80] we stabled our riding-mules in a deserted dwelling-house, and, hanging up our instruments in another, across the street from the first, made a thorough exploration of the city. We found it located on a beautiful level patch of ground, with scattering yellow pines growing all over

---

*San Juan to La Plata 1.

**Hermosa Cliffs, station 39.

+La Plata 1 to La Plata 3.

it. It was composed of one street, with a row of log cabins on either side stretching a distance of several hundred yards. Some of the houses were nearly finished, some half done, and the sites of others were marked by two or three tiers of logs laid one above the other. All were deserted. We took possession of the best-looking one, which had a kitchen attached, and made ourselves very comfortable; eating inside and sleeping out of doors. The night was so bright and clear that we could not endure sleeping under a roof. We found several persons living in the vicinity, and from them we learned that the settlers had been time and again ordered away by the Indians, and had finally considered it best to leave.

The height of this place is 6,850 feet.[81] From Baker's Park to this point, a distance of about twenty-six miles, the Animas has a fall of 2,550 feet, or an average of 100 feet to the mile.[82] Trout are found in the river here, but how abundantly I cannot say. They have never been caught as far up as Baker's Park—due, probably, to the falls between the two points.

Traveling down stream, the stream-bed soon widens into a very pretty valley, bearing the name of Animas Park. It extends from a point near Animas City, [actually near Bakers Bridge]* so-called, down the river about fourteen miles, with a maximum width of two miles. The total area may be estimated at twenty square miles, but the part capable of cultivation does not amount to more than three or four thousand acres. The greater portion of this can be irrigated at little expense. In passing through it we saw corn, wheat, potatoes, turnips, and watermelons growing finely, but all abandoned on account of Indian troubles. This valley is very interesting in many respects. First it contains almost the only tillable land within a hundred miles of the mines. Its distance from Baker's Park is only thirty-five miles by the trail. It is probably the richest little valley in the Territory, and has an elevation of only 6,700 to 6,800 feet. It faces the south, and consequently is very warm, while at the same time it is near enough to the mountains to get the benefit of their great rain-fall. Near its lower end good coal is found in the greatest abundance, while a plentiful

---

*See notes 81 & 82.

supply of good pine timber is near at hand. Farther down the river the country becomes a plain, almost perfectly barren of vegetation.

After passing through the park, we made several stations, west of the river, on low hills. On station 45,* which is not represented on the accompanying map, but situated just a little below the border,** we found some old ruins, consisting of a couple of watch-towers; one entirely disintegrated, leaving only a hole in the ground to indicate its presence, while the other still remained about four feet high, but was completely overgrown by oak-bushes. Some white and painted pottery lay about. This point is a wooded hill, east of the Rio La Plata. The day after, we found some pottery still farther north, on station 46, which is on the map.[83]

After this we followed a road which had been used by the former settlers, over to the Florida, and made several stations near that stream.† The road soon ended, and we followed its continuation, an Indian trail, to the [Los] Pinos River. This trail, by an oversight, is not represented on the map. It leaves the Animas about half a mile north of station 46, and thence crosses over to the Florida, which it follows up for several miles, then strikes across to the Pinos, and crosses that stream at the mouth of the Vallecito; crossing thence over the next ridge, it strikes the Ute trail from Los Pinos agency. It is not much used, and is consequently quite difficult to follow. There is some fine bottom-land on the Florida, capable of a high degree of cultivation, but of small extent. Near the junction of the Vallecito and Los Pinos is another small area of splendid land. These two streams running down from the quartzite peaks, carry at least one-half more water than any other streams of the same *drainage* area in the district.[84]

The next day after passing this point,†† October 2, snow began to fall, and, camping near a peak on which we had to

---

*La Plata 3 to La Plata 2, then return.

**Border of the Ute Reservation.

†La Plata 3 to La Plata 1, then return.

††La Plata 3 to Hinsdale 2.

make a station, we quietly waited for the weather to clear off.[85] By a remarkable accident we had halted in a splendid camping-place, there being none worthy the name for miles ahead of us, as we afterward found. Snow fell continuously for four days, and we found sitting in camp very hard work. On account of our peculiarly protected position the snow that fell near our camp melted as it fell, but a mile up stream it lay two feet deep. Had it not been for the good grass and shelter here offered, our worn-out mules would have fared badly. A thing worthy of note is the fact that very slight thunder and lightning continued through the whole of this snow-storm. Lieutenant Wheeler[86] narrates a similar experience in this part of the country.

On the fourth day the weather cleared off, and we succeeded in making our station, though on the summit the snow was two or three feet deep, which, with our shoes nearly worn out, was very disagreeable. Returning early from the peak we moved up the ridge. The trail being entirely hidden by the snow, we had to give it up, and after a very difficult day's march we succeeded in getting out of the snow only, and then had to camp in swampy ground, making our beds on pine boughs, which we cut from the trees. We knew now that winter had commenced, and we wanted to get out of the mountains as fast as our mules could carry us.

The next day we crossed the divide at the head of Los Pinos River, by way of the Ute trail.* The pass by this route was good, though covered with snow. In the summer it must be very easy and pleasant. We felt thankful when quite late in the afternoon we reached the Rio Grande and struck camp near the wagon-road.

The next day we traveled down the road,** which here is a very good one, to Antelope Park, which we found to be quite an extensive piece of plain country, forming here the valley of the Rio Grande, and continued below, by a narrow strip of low land, along the river. The elevation of the park is about 9,000 feet. There are several houses dotted about over it and

---

*At Weminuche Pass.

**Hinsdale 2 to Mineral 1.

farms laid out, although the elevation is too great to allow much grain to be produced.

The next day, October 9, we ascended Bristol Head and made station 54. This is a very curious bald mountain, a few miles east of Antelope Park, being the southern culminating point of a high plateau. To the east it slopes down quite gently, but on the west side it falls abruptly nearly 4,000 feet to the bottom of a very curious sink. In some places the bluff is quite vertical for over a thousand feet. Being composed of trachyte, the rock breaks off along vertical planes and gives to the precipice the character peculiar to volcanic formations. The sink already mentioned is a little valley from a quarter to half a mile broad, bordered on the east by the high bluffs of Bristol Head; and, on the west, by a ridge and bluffs reaching seven to eight hundred feet above the valley. At the lower end a narrow gate-way leads out to the Rio Grande; and, at the upper end, a beautiful lake occupies the highest part.* Just above this, Clear Creek cuts through the ridge on the west side, and flows out through Antelope Park. The whole mass of this basin has, undoubtedly, fallen in; and, at one time, Antelope Park must have jutted up against the side of the mountain.

We made the ascent of the peak from the sink, riding our mules the whole distance, except the first part of the climb, from the sink up to the ridge. On the summit we found the snow about a foot and a half deep. A large bear had left his tracks all over it. We found the slope to the east quite gradual and made the descent on that side instead of going down the way we came up.

After camping at a point on the road to the south of Bristol Head, we moved down the Rio Grande. The only place of special interest on the way was Wagon-Wheel Gap, where the river passes for a few hundred yards between two high bluffs, about 300 feet apart. This point has evidently been, in times past, a great battle-ground between the Utes and their enemies of the plains, the Cheyennes, Arapahoes, &c. Many little heaps of rocks on the south bluff seem to have done service as rifle-

---

*Now called Santa Maria Reservoir.

Bristol Head and Antelope Park. This landmark was one of the features already named in 1874, apparently by English settlers.—*Courtesy USGS, W.H. Jackson, 1874.*

pits. The toll-gate for the San Juan road is situated near this place.*

We arrived at Del Norte on October 10. The town contains several hundred inhabitants, and at the present time does a considerable business with the San Juan mines. Leaving Del Norte we traveled across San Luis Valley; far behind us we could see a new but apparently greater storm than we had yet passed through gathering around the distant mountains. Crossing over Mosca Pass and down Huerfano Park we reached Pueblo October 18.[87] The next morning we took the cars on the narrow-gauge railway, and in the evening arrived at Denver, our point of beginning.

---

*Leave Mineral County Map, Sheet 1.

NOTES

1. So they traveled about 155 miles in eleven days, or around 14 a day. That is a leisurely pace for mules, who, if pressed, can knock off well over thirty miles a day on level ground. Their riders, however, needed a break-in period.

2. All Hayden's divisions got a late start in 1874 due to the financial panic of 1873, which put the brakes on many congressional appropriations. After arriving in Saguache on July 24, Rhoda neglected specific dates until three weeks later when he climbed Handies Peak. Fortunately, Endlich's field notes date the establishment of each station. Wilson also recorded dates of most stations (Hayden's *Eighth Annual Report*, pp. 447–448); his notes agree with Endlich's. Careful map study and the experience of repeating the party's odyssey during the summer of 1982 persuaded me Endlich's calendar is the correct one. The reconstructed chronology therefore (in notes or bracketed inserts in the text) relies on Endlich. Here are their first few days after Saguache:

July 25:	resupply, start for Los Pinos Agency
July 26:	en route to the Agency
July 27:	make station 1, sleep at Agency
July 28–29:	cross Los Pinos Pass, explore Cebolla Creek
July 30:	make station 2 near Continental Divide, move to Cannibal Plateau

3. Including station 2 of 1874, San Luis Peak, Baldy Alto, and Organ Mountain.

4. The map mentioned in the text is the Preliminary Map of 1874, published, like Rhoda's *Report*, in Hayden's *Eighth Annual Report* (1876), after page 412.

5. Actually, three plateaus: Calf Creek Plateau, Cannibal Plateau, and Mesa Seco, northwest and west of Lake City.

6. Taking angles, or triangulation, is a technique of topographical surveying used in making maps. The surveyor selects three prominent points in the territory being map-

93

ped, then measures the angles between them with a theodolite, which employs a telescope that can sight horizontally or vertically. Of course, the three angles of any triangle must add up to 180 degrees. To decrease the range of error, the surveyor takes angles several times from each of the three positions, or stations, to the other two. Trigonometric calculations adjust the variances between different readings. Next, using the geometric principle that all six parts of a triangle (three sides, three angles) can be discovered if two angles and the side between them are known, the topographer figures the distances between prominent points. Since every triangle exists as part of a network of connected triangles, each calculated side becomes a known distance in an adjacent triangle. In Colorado Hayden's topographers extended their triangles from an initial baseline near Denver (later another in the San Luis Valley) that was carefully computed with a steel tape. On sketches, see note 21.

7. Writing up his report the following winter in Washington, Rhoda must have forgotten the much closer and more dramatic view from station 8, now called Crystal Peak.

8. This road crosses Cebolla Creek about three miles upstream from Powderhorn. On the Gunnison National Forest Map (1965) Forest Road 806 approximates the route from Cebolla Creek to the Old Agency Ranger Station. From there it ambles over Cochetopa Pass east into Saguache. You can draw in its likely course on county maps (Saguache 1 and Gunnison 6), but you may not find a continuous path in the field between Cebolla Creek and the Old Agency Station.

On August 3 they made station 6, and station 7 the next day.

9. This abrupt north face has never been climbed.

10. These include Redcloud Peak, Red Mountain, and several unnamed summits over 13,000 feet.

11. Colors viewed at a distance depend a great deal on atmospheric conditions, the extent of snow cover, and how re-

cently it has rained: wet rocks tend to show colors better. From Uncompahgre an observer may not discern the same kaleidoscope Rhoda saw, but he will surely find similar displays from other high places.

12. "Uncompahgre Mountains" refers to the summits stretching from around Mount Sneffels north-northeast through Wetterhorn and Uncompahgre Peaks and east nearly to the Lake Fork. Seen from the north, these peaks serve as the first sentinels of the San Juan Mountains, though neither geologically nor geographically do they deserve designation as a separate range. Modern maps no longer show the "Uncompahgre Mountains."

13. Godwin [Henson] Creek, by the way, commemorates Charles Godwin (or Goodwin) and Henry Henson. In partnership with two others, they discovered the rich Ute-Ulay Mine west of Lake City in 1871. Godwin may have been the more prominent originally, suggested by the priority of his name in association with this creek, but obscurity swallowed him. Henson later became a judge. A town named for him near the Ute-Ulay Mine flourished from 1880–93.

14. The "pretty extensive plateau" centers on American Flats, though in enlarging it from Wetterhorn Peak (the "high, sharp pinnacle a few miles west of Uncompahgre Peak") south to the vicinity of Cinnamon Pass, Rhoda over-simplified. Instead of a single plateau, a better description would be a series of lofty basins and plateaus subtending a dominant ridge, suggestive of vertebrae branching off a spinal column.

15. Assuming Rhoda still speaks of pinnacles near Mount Sneffels, he understates the distance from his perch on station 10: closer to ten miles, depending on the pinnacles viewed.

16. Henry G. Prout, an assistant engineer with the U.S. Topographical Engineers, was in charge of field work for Lt. E. H. Ruffner's expedition during the summer of 1873. Ute Indians and white explorers had been quarreling over the location of the eastern boundary of the Ute reservation

(107th meridian). Ruffner's job was to cool the dispute with some reliable information. Before the year's end, however, the question became irrelevant. See note 29.

17. The mud slides began after the Wisconsin glaciation (within the last ten thousand years). The most recent slippage—to judge by the bent trees—has been during the lives of existing trees.

18. John A. Randolph, on assignment for *Harper's Weekly*, found the bodies near Cannibal Plateau. In 1873 Alferd E. Packer (that's his spelling of the first name) hired on as a guide for several adventurers from Utah. Reaching the San Juan mining area in the dead of winter, most of the group opted to sit tight until spring. The five who couldn't wait encountered bad weather, ran out of supplies, and were apparently killed and eaten by Packer— giving rise to the story (untrue but noteworthy) that at his trial years later the judge condemned Packer for eating half the Democrats of Hinsdale County.

19. Either on Redcloud Peak (14,034 feet) or Sunshine Peak (14,001 feet). In the following narrative Wilson and Rhoda climbed Sunshine and established station 12 there. Endlich, the geologist, was working simultaneously on the slopes of Redcloud.

20. Snare Creek still flows, but no longer as the principal tributary, having been replaced in that capacity by Cottonwood Creek, of which Snare Creek now is a secondary tributary.

21. The topographer sketched the countryside to show drainages, elevations (using contours), and the appearance of features between the specific points located with the theodolite. Simultaneously, the geologist drew in with different colors the extent of various formations and showed their relationships in vertical sections. Both sets of sketches contributed directly to the final maps of the territory.

22. In Greek mythology, the musician who played his lyre so sweetly that stones followed him.

23. Mercurial barometers give an indication of altitude, be-

cause the level of mercury in a column responds directly to atmospheric pressure, which varies proportionally to altitude. They also respond to changes in weather, making them unreliable as altimeters. Hayden's men understood this and tried to take many readings from each location to average out the errors.

Vertical angles taken with the theodolite provide more precision. Instruments with an eight-inch circle read to five-second gradations, making for high accuracy. Even the more common four-inch circles read to a minute of arc (1/60 of a degree). Unfortunately, afternoon thunderstorms rarely permitted time for both horizontal and vertical triangulation. Thus barometers were used, and thus Hayden's elevations require correcting, though not often by more than 100 feet.

Another informal way of estimating elevations, hypsometry, involved noting the time required to boil a constant amount of water, which decreases proportionally to altitude.

24. Topographers built monuments with stones, often six to eight feet tall, on the top of many high stations. The monuments provided a sighting target for the theodolite when viewed from other summits in the triangulation system. Few of these genuine artifacts survive, since later mountaineers destroyed them, unaware of their historic value. One of the best survivors bestrides Cannibal Plateau, north of Powderhorn Lakes.

25. Two Negroes worked for Hayden in Colorado, Judge Porter and William Shaw. I am not sure which accompanied Wilson's division in 1874.

26. A shallow iron pot or kettle which absorbed heat from the fire directly beneath it as well as from burning coals heaped on its lid.

27. A. C. Peale, another of Hayden's men, described them best: "The saddles or 'aparejos' are made of stout leather stuffed with hay and kept in shape by a framework of willow sticks. When on the ground in line before the picket rope they look like a row of huge stuffed saddlebags stand-

ing on end. They are about three feet high and have broad cruppers and breast straps. When put on the mule they are covered with *mantas* [blankets], made of coarse matting, which are secured by wide canvas cinches or girths. These also bind the aparejo to the mule." (*Illustrated Christian Weekly*, August 26, 1876.)

28. Handies probably was an early settler.

29. A few bold sourdoughs had been poking around the San Juans since the 1860s, but the Brunot Treaty of September 13, 1873—which transferred most of the San Juan Mountains from the Ute Indians to the United States—opened the door to serious development. Hayden ordered Wilson's division to the San Juan region in the spring of 1874 largely to study its mineralogical potential before the expected flood of miners poured in.

30. Though not precisely delineated by Rhoda, who only climbed on the fringes of the group, the quartzites include the Grenadier Range and part of the Needle Mountains. They stretch from west of the Animas River (e.g., Snowdon Peak or station 38) to beyond Vallecito Creek on the southeast (e.g., Mount Oso, or station 23). Typically blue-gray in color, they present steep and continuous faces.

31. Mount Eolus, which Rhoda included in the quartzite peaks, was named for the Greek father of the winds. Confined to bags, the winds escaped only upon the whim of Eolus–not a bad description of weather in the Chicago Basin.

32. Enos Hotchkiss and Otto Mears brought the toll road from Saguache that same year, 1874. Earlier in the year, Hotchkiss had uncovered a good mine near Lake San Cristobal, news of which attracted numerous others. Before the year was out, booming Lake City boasted of concentrators (for washing impurities out of ore) and smelters (for burning out more resistant ones). A year later it possessed a sawmill, sixty-seven finished buildings, a newspaper (*Silver World*), about 600 people, and had snatched the primacy of Hinsdale County from San Juan City (the first county seat, located in Antelope Park on the Rio Grande).

An indirect connection to Silverton came in 1877 when Lake City investors pushed a road up Henson Creek that crossed the divide at both Engineer Pass and Yvonne Pass. From there it wandered south to Mineral Point, then over Denver Pass and down to Animas Forks and Silverton. Later Hotchkiss built a more direct line up the Lake Fork to Cinnamon Pass.

33. Station 15, August 16.

34. Several times during the Pleistocene epoch the Animas Canyon hosted mighty glaciers, evidence of which Rhoda noticed here in the hanging valleys. Later he saw the same in Cunningham Gulch, where he described the amphitheatrical shape of valleys so characteristic of the San Juan Mountains. Rhoda thought that shape had something to do with the ubiquitous volcanic rock. He was right, but for the wrong reasons. He thought the yawning valleys were due to a sinking of the earth's crust, not realizing the awesome effects of prolonged glacial sculpting in soft volcanic tuff. Significantly, while it tentatively acknowledged glacial evidence across the San Juans, Endlich's geological report similarly misunderstood the deep amphitheaters. Even this mistake, however, emphasizes the historical value of Rhoda's essay. The concept of glacial geology had only recently been introduced, largely by the Swiss-American Louis Agassiz (1807–73), and it was not yet universally accepted or understood. To study modern geological reports is to realize that virtually all the high peaks Rhoda climbed in 1874 were once surrounded by deep glaciers.

35. Charles Baker probably discovered the park during the summer of 1860, when he arrived as the harbinger of a large group of fortune hunters from Denver, who came on the next winter. The party quarreled, split up, and Baker headed back east, in time to enlist in the Confederate army. After the war, he returned to the park that bears his name, only to be killed by Indians in 1868.

36. Major Cunningham headed a party from Chicago that searched for minerals here and later formed a syndicate to invest in the mines.

37. Howardsville became the county seat of La Plata County in 1874, the first such on the Western Slope, then promptly surrendered the honor to Silverton the following year (San Juan County was not organized until 1876). A Lt. Howard came to the site in 1860 with Charles Baker, but his progenitor's role is disputed by supporters of George W. Howard, a miner who built his home there in 1871.

38. After Rhoda's first visit, but before the year had passed, Howardsville gained its own mail service. Mail from Del Norte originally arrived via Cunningham Pass, not Stony Pass. See note 54.

39. On that point did Mr. Rhoda err. King Solomon Mountain is, and was in 1874, south of Howardsville.

40. No, 3,400 feet in 7,000 horizontal feet. Rhoda's vertical measurements, made with the barometer, are close. That his horizontal distances miss the mark shows he relied on his own eye here, rather than the results of triangulation. Like every other experienced mountaineer in the world, Rhoda underestimated distance in the unfamiliar alpine world.

41. If we take Cascade (northeast of Electra Lake) as "the lower end of the great canon," it is thirty miles traveling along the riverbed from Animas Forks. A crow's flight between Handies Peak and Mount Eolus would cover twenty-one miles. Hayden's parties often calculated distances along streams and roads, but I doubt that anyone in Rhoda's group did so for the Animas. Rhoda probably collected this accurate figure from local hearsay.

42. Today cartographers distinguish a Kendall Mountain (13,066 feet) and adjoining Kendall Peak (13,481 feet). Rhoda obviously refers to the latter. James Kendall had been in Bakers Park as early as 1871, and his name already adorned the summit when Rhoda arrived.

43. Brand new, having been organized just this year.

44. Not so. Cement Creek flows mostly from north to south.

45. That is, from the mouth of Mineral Creek to Cascade, which is about seventeen miles.

46. Quartzite crops out in the surrounding Needle Mountains and in the canyon, but schists and gneisses form the principal rocks of the canyon walls.

47. Rhoda's perplexity here has an interesting history. Geologists at the time realized the gouging character of rivers and glaciers, though they still expressed amazement that mere water or ice might cut thousands of feet through rock "as hard as steel." Enter the concept of the antecedent stream, which, to quote a modern geological dictionary, "was established before local uplift began and incised its channel at the same rate the land was rising." In other words, the energy creating many dramatic canyon walls came partly from the cutting action of the river, but also from upthrusting forces in the earth's crust. John Wesley Powell took credit for originating the idea of antecedent streams in 1875, but two years earlier Hayden had announced it in different words. (See Hayden's *Sixth Annual Report* (1873), p. 85.)

48. Once again, Rhoda underestimated how rapidly transportation would develop. An engine of the Denver and Rio Grande Railroad steamed up Animas Canyon and into Silverton during July 1882. Its early arrival was prompted by a need for efficient access to the smelters in Durango.

49. Today it is the most heavily used, ironically enough, thanks to modern engineering and a heroic highway department. This is US 550 south to Durango, over Molas Pass (10,899 feet) and Coal Bank Pass (10,660 feet).

50. The route ascended modern Bear Creek to its source at the pass, just under two miles southwest of Sultan Mountain. It then descended southeast and joined the first egress Rhoda mentions in the vicinity of Molas Pass.

51. Like the previous pass, this one bears no name on recent maps and is ascended on a faint hiking trail. Bear Creek of Rhoda's day is the South Fork of Mineral Creek on today's maps. The pass (at 12,445 feet) looms about two miles west-southwest above Bandora Mine, and a bit over a mile south of Beattie Peak along the ridge. It drops down to

Lake Fork of the San Miguel by way of Lake Hope and Trout Lake.

52. Otto Mears was not intimidated by this precipitous box canyon, and after spending $10,000 per mile opened a road in 1884 between Ouray and Silverton. Tourists call it the "Million Dollar Highway."

    The trail to the second pass over to the Uncompahgre headwaters followed Cement Creek to Gladstone, topped out just northwest of Hurricane Peak, then descended to Lake Como and Poughkeepsie Gulch.

53. The figure 12,900 is clearly a misprint. He gives 12,090 later on, which is within ten feet of present estimates.

54. Most writers have assumed this to be Stony Pass (12,588 feet)—incorrectly. From the elevation and description he gives (pp. 45-46), Rhoda certainly used another pass a mile and a half south of Stony, which he later calls Cunningham Pass. Others called it Rio Grande Pass. In the early years it carried its share of the freight, perhaps most of it to judge by Rhoda's next sentence. Its steepness and perpetual muddiness doubtless explains why in 1879 it was superseded by a toll road over Stony Pass. The route Rhoda used is delineated on the San Juan Forest Map (1974).

55. Having mentioned seven passes, why elevation gains for only five? Because Rhoda regarded the two to the north through Uncompahgre Canyon as impractical. The five, with his elevations (given later in an appendix), he called: pass east of Sultan Mountain (10,460 feet); pass west of Sultan Mountain (11,570 feet); Bear Creek Pass (12,600 feet); Lake Fork Pass [Cinnamon] (12,540 feet); and Cunningham Pass (12,090 feet).

56. The Spanish devised the arrastra as a circular stone trough for grinding ore. A large, smoothed rock supplied the crushing force, and a mule supplied the power to drag the rock around and around. An arrastra was built and used in this gulch by early prospectors. The first mine in Bakers Park opened in Arrastra Gulch in 1870. Called the

Little Giant, it worked one of the few gold veins in this part of the San Juans. Silver was king, and its common ore, galena, contained lead that miners first separated in crushing mills, powered by the numerous waterfalls Rhoda observed in the park.

57. Rhoda's chronology now agrees with Endlich's again.

58. Notably Table Mountain and Snow Mesa. The Continental Divide is just south of station 2.

59. What puzzled Rhoda from station 19 was the abrupt appearance of Bristol Head, a problem to which he gave a wrong solution later when describing the country west of Bristol Head around Clear Creek. See also note 34.

60. Rhoda meant to say Lost Trail Creek here, instead of Pole Creek; thus, the packtrain had gone up Ute Creek. They camped that night near the junction of Middle Ute Creek and East Ute Creek.

61. Indeed, another surveyor! A party of the Geographical Surveys of the Territories West of the 100th Meridian (1869–79), under the direction of Lt. George Montague Wheeler, had already reached the summit that very summer and used it as one of their triangulation stations. Wheeler's survey in Colorado, led by Lt. William L. Marshall, overlapped with Hayden's on several stations.

62. Rhoda worked out this accurate distance by triangulation.

63. Probably Storm King Peak, 13,752 feet.

64. Really two days ago, on August 24 when returning from Mount Oso. Rhoda forgot the day they spent in camp, and he muddles the chronology after breaking camp on Middle Ute Creek August 26. Again Endlich's notes come to the rescue, and in his diary W. H. Jackson says he met Wilson's group in Howardsville on the 28th. So on the 26th they descended from the Continental Divide to Rock Creek, then set up camp on a branch of the Vallecito, probably Nebo Creek. On the 27th they reascended the divide in the vicinity of Hunchback Pass, made station 24, and camped on upper Bear Creek. On the 28th they climbed White Dome (not Mount Nebo, as some have thought), as station 25, then

rode along the divide to the Cunningham Pass trail, which they followed down to Howardsville.

65. More accurately, the northeast: from White Dome to around Mount Oso.

66. Jackson's diary records that he made a side trip with Wilson and Rhoda during August 29–31 while awaiting supplies from San Juan City. On the 29th they got a late start and camped at the foot of Sultan Mountain, which they started up the next day but were driven back to camp by storms. They reached the summit August 31, from which Jackson took a number of pictures. Wilson and Rhoda used Sultan Mountain (station 26) as a "common datum-point," from which to compare the heights of other surrounding stations. Jackson spent September 1 taking pictures of Wilson's party in and around Howardsville. Supplies arrived that day, so on September 2 both divisions went their separate ways.

67. Rhoda descended Red Mountain Pass by Red Mountain Creek, not the Uncompahgre itself, the head of which geographers locate several miles east in Poughkeepsie Gulch.

68. See note 51 on this pass.

69. The coloration is due to veins of hematite (the dull red) and pyrite (yellow) along the ridge. Geologically, this area offers great interest with three distinct sedimentary formations, two volcanic flows, glacial moraine, and evidence of landslides.

70. This unnamed drainage separates Ruffner Mountain from Iron Mountain.

71. An aerie (about 13,200 feet) perhaps a mile east of Mears Peak. Undoubtedly, Wilson chose the most difficult approach to Mount Sneffels.

72. The etymology is instructive. During the climb one member of the party remarked on the similarity of the deep basin of Blue Lakes to the great crater in Jules Verne's *Journey to the Center of the Earth* (1864). Rising to the

literary bait, Endlich said, pointing at the peak, "Yes, and there's Sneffels," referring to the Icelandic volcano (Snaefellsjökull) immortalized by Verne's novel.

73. On a clear day the view from Sneffels is remarkable, but Rhoda exaggerates. Of the thirty-two stations made so far, he probably saw only eighteen. Most of those below 13,000 feet would have been obscured by intervening ridges and peaks.

74. The La Sal Mountains lie northwest of Sneffels. Rhoda probably referred to the Sierra Abajo. Both ranges reside in Utah.

75. What he saw to the north and northwest were Grand Mesa, the Elk Mountains, and the Sawatch Range.

76. Named for Allen D. Wilson, leader of this expedition, whose name also identifies Wilson Peak (14,017 feet), a mile and a half to the northwest.

77. Hereafter Rhoda again becomes indifferent to chronology. The next two weeks are as follows:

Sept. 14:   make station 36
Sept. 15:   make station 37, return to Mineral Creek via Bear Creek [South Fork] Pass
Sept. 16:   reach Howardsville
Sept. 17–18: in Howardsville
Sept. 19:   start down the Animas River
Sept. 20:   make station 38
Sept. 21:   make station 39
Sept. 22:   explore Animas River below great canyon
Sept. 23:   make station 40, arrive in Animas City
Sept. 24:   make station 41 on Perins Peak
Sept. 25:   make stations 42 & 43
Sept. 26:   make station 44 above Horse Gulch
Sept. 27:   explore lower Animas, find ruins southwest of Durango, make station 45
Sept. 28:   find more pottery near Durango at station 46, move to Florida River, make station 47
Sept. 29:   explore Florida River
Sept. 30:   makes stations 48 & 49

Oct. 1:   move to the Los Pinos River; above its junction with Vallecito Creek make station 50

78. Jackson's diary shows he traveled with Wilson's party for the five days, September 19–23.

79. Snowdon Peak, named for Francis M. Snowden (note spelling variation), who built the first cabin in Silverton in 1874.

80. The site of Animas City lies within modern Durango, near the northern edge of town. Miners organized it in 1873. Seven years later the Denver and Rio Grande Railroad built Durango two miles south.

81. This elevation for Animas Park is wrong, because either Rhoda or the printer, or both, inadvertently placed Animas City some fifteen miles too far north at Bakers Bridge, where the elevation is indeed about 6,850 feet.

82. Also inaccurate, but consistent with the error of placing Animas City too far north (see note 81). The river does drop about 2,550 feet between Bakers Park and Bakers Bridge, though the distance is thirty miles along the river and thirty-five via the road. Notice that Rhoda corrects the distance in the next paragraph to thirty-five miles.

83. This is the best place to correct the most blatant errors which crept into the Preliminary Map concerning stations. Numbers 43, 45, & 50 are omitted; then, for good measure, two stations 46 appear. The northernmost of the two stations 46 should be 43. Number 45 is located by both the *Atlas* and Rhoda's tables in the same place. Station 50, however, is missing on all four sources I used to locate the other stations, and it eluded me until I found at the Field Records Office of the USGS in Denver a series of hand-drawn maps, apparently assembled from field notes and used to prepare the printed maps of the *Atlas*. I noticed that pin holes perforated the maps at all the stations, and a very few other prominent points, as if someone had once placed markers on these pins for easy reference. The only pin hole between stations 49 & 51 appears in a place tolerably consistent with Endlich's notes, just southwest

of station 51 atop Granite Peak. This map also enabled me to confirm the other stations, especially the questionable placements of 52 and 53 on the Preliminary Map.

84. This is more than Rhoda's own hunch. Hayden's many assignments to his field parties included gauging streams.

85. Their last days passed as follows:

Oct. 2:	try to make another station, but storm intervenes
Oct. 3:	in camp, snowstorm
Oct. 4:	ditto
Oct. 5:	ditto
Oct. 6:	snow ceases, make station 51, move up Los Pinos River
Oct. 7:	make station 52 across river from station 22, cross Weminuche Pass to the upper Rio Grande River
Oct. 8:	make station 53 above Rio Grande, move downstream to Antelope Park
Oct. 9:	ascend Bristol Head (station 54)
Oct. 10:	continue down river, pass Wagon Wheel Gap, reach Del Norte.

86. Lieutenant G. M. Wheeler. See note 61.

87. It may surprise the motorist that a week elapsed between Del Norte and Pueblo, for their journey, of about 140 miles, crossed only one mountain pass. Considering that they established eleven more stations along the way, however, and still averaged 20 miles a day, they moved as fast as possible.

Franklin Rhoda, about twenty years old—*Courtesy Pauline Vieira.*

FRANK RHODA

Some of the most colorful characters in history have rambled and strutted across this earthly stage in the theatre of the American West. Their dramatics stand out even in the longer run of global history for extravagance and versatility. Often ignored in their own day, they thoroughly captured the imagination of later generations, who seem soft by comparison, if not downright effete.

For those who rejoice in the discovery of these mavericks, it is a pleasure to introduce Franklin Rhoda (often called Frank), a man whose outrageous deeds and unfulfilled dreams well qualify him for a place in the pantheon of forgotten Western heroes.

An adventurous life might have been foretold for the son of Frederick Rhoda, who in 1850 had traveled from the Missouri River to the Pacific Coast via the Oregon Trail. For the next nine and a half years the family roamed between British Columbia and San Francisco before finally settling in Fruitvale (now part of East Oakland), where Frederick acquired acreage for fruit orchards. Franklin was born on June 14, 1854 in Crescent City, California.[1]

A member of the first class to graduate from the University of California in July 1873, at the age of nineteen, Franklin wrote a "History of the Class of '73" in which he foreshadowed his literary gifts.

> After four years we are suddenly stopped in our onward course, like the sediment of a fast flowing river when it reaches the sea, when the checking of its velocity causes it to settle down. So we may be fast now, but sooner or later we will be checked and forced to settle down, and like the aforesaid sediment we may deposit in a bank or start a bar, according to the amount of liquid present and the size of the check.[2]

He also gave warning of his religious predilictions, complaining that "none of the professors could pray," and elaborating, "if there by any in '73 who are lax in their devotion to religion,

it should be ascribed to early training in this branch of education of such dreadful import to all ungodly sinners." But he
managed to disguise his zeal beneath an affable humor.

> Notwithstanding all these facts the members of the class were
> not long in finding out that they still had a religious function
> to perform, besides their statical moral effect. They soon dis-
> covered that their *forte* lay in the conversion of poor, deluded,
> intoxicated, worldly sinners to the rectilinear pathos of righte-
> ousness, and how well they defended their *forte* the sequel will
> tell. First of all, like the discreet missionaries they were, they
> sought to learn the ways of the wicked, in order the more
> effectually to combat that old Saurian monster, "Sin."

Shortly after graduation, Rhoda traveled to Colorado to join
his half brother, Allen D. Wilson, who was in charge of one
of Hayden's surveying divisions. For the next three summers
he cultivated a practical knowledge of the civil engineering he
had studied in Berkeley. He harvested the fruit of that labor
in his *Report*. The next year he penned a review of the 1875
season, which lacks the historical importance of the 1874 report
but sparkles with the same wit and insight.[3]
From the scientific viewpoint one can only regret that Rhoda
did not follow Wilson in a career of engineering. Let each
reader judge the talent of this rawboned youth by comparing
two of his field sketches with a finished drawing of the more
mature William Henry Holmes, deemed the greatest topographical artist of his day. (Compare figures 11 and 15 with
5.) Fate had dealt him other cards, however. After 1876 he
helped his father for a few years with the orchards, but in
1880 he took a step that revealed his heart's desire and set the
course of his life. On December 12 he organized a Sunday
school in Fruitvale, and he conducted it faithfully until October
1884, when he moved to San Francisco.[4]
During this time he published in October 1881 a small book
entitled *Bible Gems*. It is a compilation of some favorite biblical
quotations, which he used in teaching at the Sunday school.
In August 1882 he prepared a special edition of the book, "for
the professors, students, and alumni of the University of Califor-

nia," and deposited it in the library at Berkeley. The forword, addressed to members of the university community, reveals an inner turmoil and searching.

> Having been myself rescued from the power of sin, through the love and mercy of Jesus Christ, I have long had an earnest desire to do something that might recommend Him to my friends of the University of California....
>
> I trust that all who have tried to post themselves on the current learning of the day, have found that no amount of learning will give us the mastery over the simplest bad habit, how much less purge the records of our past lives from guilt. Having tried by many devices to rid myself from evil and to live an honest and upright life, and having for years been baffled in every attempt, in sheer despair I turned to the much disused and neglected Bible, and by earnest prayer, found a Savior who was able to save to the uttermost.
>
> Now I know that in the University, with all its literary and scientific training the Bible is a disused book. I speak from personal experience. It is to supply this lack to some extent at least, that I desire to present you this little book of Bible Gems.

An energetic revivalist bandwagon rolled through Oakland and San Francisco in the 1870s and 1880s, and Rhoda jumped aboard.[5] He worked with the Salvation Army, and he supported a splinter group of the Christian Scientists who taught faith healing.[6] Many people dismissed him as another religious crank, but they underestimated the man. In addition to a profound conviction that spread contagiously, Rhoda brought to religion the same scholarly temperament he applied to topography. He read Greek and Hebrew, and he studied ancient texts before preparing his sermons and writings.[7] Between May and October 1884, in association with W.A. Spurlock, Rhoda co-edited and wrote a series of religious articles which they distributed free in newspaper form. In September 1885 he and Spurlock brought out a monthly newspaper, *The Father's Love*, which ran until November 1886. His articles show wide familiarity with Old and New Testaments and an original combination of biblical references to drive home a message of individual redemption. He also advocated social ideas that no doubt embarrassed the more churchy Christians: tolerate the Chinese, recognize the rights of women, reconcile with the Jews, embrace communism.

> In the extremes to which professing Christians have gone in toadying to wealth they have covered up a most significant fact, that the promulgation of the Gospel by Jesus began with communism, and is to end in it.... In holiness, communism finds its ultimate fulfillment. When sin is destroyed out of the world, and holiness covers the earth, then, and not till then, can communism become universal. In holiness, communism becomes brotherly love. He that fulfills the command to love his neighbor as himself must be a communist.[8]

While this radicalism was driving his life, Rhoda remained close to one traditional form of religious expression, and displayed another facet of his brilliant character, by encouraging an appreciation of music in his congregations. He was a skilled organist, and arranged at least one religious song during the 1880s, "Jesus Now Is Coming," in seven verses.[9]

During the late 1880s he moderated his views, and his behavior changed accordingly. He broke with the pseudo Christian Scientists. In 1888 he sailed to China and spent several months there visiting missions. He entered San Francisco Theological Seminary at San Anselmo, graduated in 1889, and was ordained by the Presbytery of San Francisco the same year. In 1890 he married Bessie Williams, fifteen years his junior, and settled down in San Francisco to begin accommodating himself to the less apocalyptic visions of the established church. As the Rhodas moved into a series of different houses to keep pace with the family's growth, Franklin held pastorates at the Memorial Presbyterian Church in San Francisco, 1889–92, and the Valona Presbyterian Church in Crockett, 1895–99. That he had lost none of his fervor while holding church office, however, he demonstrated in the years between by working as an evangelist in San Francisco, moving about, preaching wherever he could gain an audience.[10]

His reconciliation with respectability was completed in 1899 with his election as pastor of Fruitvale Presbyterian Church.

Rhoda had come full circle: the church was only a short distance from the patrimonial orchards where he had grown up, and since Fruitvale Presbyterian was the direct successor to the Sunday school he had founded there in 1880, his promotion was a personal rendition of the return of the prodigal son.

For the next seventeen years he devoted himself to this small, almost rural parish. The results bespeak his characteristic energy and creativity. At its highest, church membership nearly tripled during his tenure, and available funding more than doubled.[11] Rhoda identified needy groups and mobilized a growing relief for their benefit. He reorganized and enlarged the volunteer societies within the congregation. He encouraged a missionary policy committing his parish to share in an international effort by the Presbyterian Church. He cooperated with ministers from nearby churches, and he invited a singing evangelist to spend three weeks rejuvenating his flock. He saw to the hiring of an organist, and he recruited a choir. Above all he sought through his own words to instill in his parishioners a grasp of the Word so fundamental to his own life. He preached at two services nearly every Sunday in the year. He led prayer meetings before services (sometimes separate ones for men and women), prayer meetings on Wednesday evenings, evening services and song services scores of times throughout the year, often in private homes. In addition he sometimes held special meetings during the week before communion services, or all day meetings on Thanksgiving day.

Rhoda retired from Fruitvale in 1916, and though he served for short periods at both the First Presbyterian Church of Oakland and the Point Arena Presbyterian Church, his interests branched out, and, like the roots of the fruit trees he loved so much, sought those nutrients hidden from common observation. Local history became the passion of these years, and he assembled thoughts and discoveries for his neighbors in Fruitvale in numerous newspaper articles.[12]

His keen eye and searching mind kept pace with his restless feet, and the three collaborated on portraits of the people, events, and natural settings of Alameda County. Henderson Luelling, the man who brought fruit trees to the East Bay in 1856, was a favorite subject. John Charles Frémont was another. Rhoda located the spot from which Frémont, at the autumnal equinox in 1845, had seen the setting sun drop exactly into the gap between the promontories of the coastal range that he named Chrysopylae, or Golden Gate. Rhoda's poetic insight shines out in these later essays, never more so than when describing a natural event.

> I suppose everyone who has one spark of romance or poetry has felt the subtle influences that come from the ceaseless motion and endless dashing of the breakers on the shore. As I listen it seems as if the hoary ocean were struggling to speak to ears too dull to hear. It seems like some great mystery that you strain to hear and comprehend, but which eternally eludes you.[13]

In his chosen words every writer betrays a bit of his own predicaments, and Rhoda was no exception.

> I like the idea of making a park of the redwoods, but when I think of this poor tax-stricken town I wish some one, who happens to have surplus wealth, and is meditating cursing his progeny by passing it on to them in bulk, would buy the land and donate it to the city in their honor.[14]

He had inherited comfortably from his father's orchards and financial success, but, being an idealist who scorned money, Rhoda husbanded his ample resources poorly, and they gradually dwindled. He chose to follow the scriptural admonitions of charity rather than those of fruitfulness, but the anxiety he felt about exercising that choice is captured in the quotation.

A final quote so perfectly embodies his unique interests that it will serve as Franklin Rhoda's epitaph and the conclusion of this brief biography.

> All this leads me to remark that the Creator has written two books. One is formed of letters and words, the other of leaves and flowers, and trees and water, and air and rock, and rain and snow, and sunshine and stars and cloud, the thunder, the cyclone and the earthquake. Some read one book, some the other. Most people read neither, nor desire to learn even the alphabet. One book is the complement of the other. He who

reads one to the neglect of the other has only a one-sided development. The prophets and apostles, like their Master, were exceedingly familiar with nature.[15]

Rhoda died September 10, 1929 of a heart attack, at the age of seventy-five. When he collapsed, he had been working in his garden.

Notes

1. Rev. Franklin Rhoda, "Auto-Biographical Sketch," a typescript written June 29, 1922, in Point Arena, California; available through the Library of the California Historical Society.

2. *Oakland Daily Transcript*, July 13, 1873, page 3.

3. "Topographical Report of the Southeastern Division," which is in F.V. Hayden, *Ninth Annual Report of the United States Geological and Geographical Survey of the Territories* (Washington, 1877).

4. Fruitvale Presbyterian Church, Oakland, Session Book One, "History of Fruitvale Presbyterian Church," facing page 1.

5. Joseph Eugene Baker, *Past and Present of Alameda County* (Chicago, 1914), I, 314, & ff.

6. Details on his religious activities will be found in my article, "A Light of the World—Rev. Franklin Rhoda and Bay Area Presbyterianism, 1880-1916." *Journal of Presbyterian History*, Vol. 62, No. 2 (Summer 1984).

7. Interview with Pauline Vieira (Mrs. Gerald J. Vieira), Rhoda's granddaughter, on August 20, 1983.

8. "The Communist Gate," *The Everlasting Gospel* (Oakland), August 15, 1884, page 1. Available in the University of California Library, Berkeley, "Articles on Various Subjects, by Franklin Rhoda, Class of '73."

9. The song is located near the end of the unpaginated source cited in note 8.

10. Dates of pastorates confirmed in correspondence with Mary Plummer, the Presbyterian Historical Society, 425 Lombard Street, Philadelphia, PA 19147.

11. This and the following information is based on the original Minutes of Session and Minutes of the Board of Trustees, Fruitvale Presbyterian Church.

12. Not all of them survive, but I have used what exists in the Bancroft Library and the several articles in the family's possession, which Pauline Vieira was kind enough to copy for me.

13. "Tramping Through Sonoma County," *Oakland Weekly News*, July 3, 1914.

14. "Some Historic Trees," *Dimond News*, June 25, 1923.

15. "That Stroll," *Dimond News*, March 17, 1924.

Allen D. Wilson, in the middle 1870s, about thirty years old—*Courtesy American Heritage Center, University of Wyoming.*

A.D. WILSON

As one of the foremost geographers and mountaineers of the nineteenth century, A.D. Wilson deserves to be better known. Let's start by knowing him correctly: he was Allen Wilson, not Ada Wilson as a couple of books have it, and the middle name was David, not Davis, as one article has it. Family papers specify the middle name, and official records consistently identify him as Allen D. Wilson.

He was born in Sparta, Illinois on September 17, 1844, the second son of a Mr. Wilson and Elizabeth Donaldson Wilson. Mr. Wilson died soon after Allen's birth, and his widow supported herself by teaching school. She moved to Iowa and was teaching school there when she met and married Frederick Rhoda in the winter of 1849–50. He was also the father of two sons, from a marriage that had ended in divorce.

In the spring of 1850 Frederick Rhoda, his new wife, and her two sons left Council Bluffs, Iowa for the Northwest via the Oregon Trail. They arrived at the future site of Portland ninety-nine days later, then moved south to the Rogue River region, setting up residence temporarily at Tattar Gulch near Sailor Diggings, where the family prospected for gold until they were chased away by Indians. The Rhoda's first son, Albert, was born here in 1851. The family's next stopping place of any duration was Crescent City, California, another mining boom town, where Franklin Rhoda was born in 1854. While there, Frederick got in the habit of buying an extra cow whenever he could. He sold some to the miners for beef, and kept others for their milk, which was also sold.

About 1856, as the prospecting faded, the family moved to Chico in the Sacramento Valley and established themselves in the cattle business. "Fever and ague" (probably malaria) began taking a toll of the residents, and young Franklin was so sick his father brought him briefly to the San Francisco Bay area, where the ocean air restored him to health. Returning to Chico, the family decided to move on, and they drove their cattle southwest into Sonoma County, where they stayed nearly a year.

About 1858 they began a cattle drive north across Oregon Territory to Lillooet, British Columbia. Located on the Fraser River, this community was the hub of another mining dig, and the family set up a butcher shop to feed the miners. But after two years they decided it was time to renounce the wayfaring life. They took a steamer to San Francisco, crossed the Bay, bought orchard land from Alfred Luelling, and put down roots during December 1860 in what became Fruitvale. By then young Allen Wilson was sixteen. During these early years he had become an expert horseman, and had shown a taste for adventure. He had also displayed a remarkable skill in finding his way in the wilds.[1]

While helping his stepfather with the orchards, Wilson took some formal education at nearby Oakland College School.[2] Also known as Brayton College, after Rev. Isaac H. Brayton who had been its principal since 1859 and its owner since 1864, the school existed to train young boys to enter the College of California as soon as they were ready and the college could be built. By 1860 the school enrolled between sixty and seventy students, and the oldest of them were ready in that year to begin collegiate studies. Ties between the institutions remained close: for example, Brayton became Professor of Rhetoric for the college in May 1860, while continuing as principal of the school. The college began graduating students in 1864, but then in 1869 transferred its property and rights to the newly formed University of California.[3] The Oakland College School continued, and Rhoda prepared for admission to the university there.

Meanwhile, Wilson did not stay long enough at the college to graduate. He left during 1867 and in March hired on as an assistant topographer with the Geological Survey of California.[4] Working under Charles Francis Hoffmann, Wilson learned the art of surveying by triangulation and mastered Hoffmann's special techniques for extending continuous triangles across alpine country. Two others who learned along with Wilson were James Terry Gardner and Clarence King.

In 1868 the Survey's director, Josiah Dwight Whitney, could not garner sufficient sponsorship from the California legislature to undertake field work. Wilson and Hoffmann went off on a private survey at Santa Barbara, and made an examination of the "oil region" there for Whitney.[5] While the California Survey was encountering political roadblocks, Clarence King decided there was room for another survey, and in 1867 he got the sponsorship of the War Department to begin his U.S. Geological Exploration of the Fortieth Parallel. When field work ran out for the California Survey, Wilson needed something to do, and by July of 1868 he had joined King as assistant topographer to Samuel Franklin Emmons in Nevada.[6]

Wilson worked with King for five seasons, 1868–72, spending the winters in Washington helping to prepare maps and publications. His companions included King's closest friend, J.T. Gardner, who now was chief topographer for the Fortieth Parallel Survey. During these years Wilson worked in eastern California, across Nevada and Utah, and into western Colorado, southern Wyoming, and southeastern Idaho. In 1870, on a swing to the Pacific Northwest to study volcanoes and glaciers, he and S.F. Emmons made their mark as mountaineers by becoming only the second party to reach the summit of Mount Ranier.[7] Though he was subordinate to Gardner, everyone recognized Wilson's ability, and his duties as topographer often equaled Gardner's.

Certainly the most dramatic part of his work with King came in the autumn of 1872, when he and others of King's Survey successfully exposed the infamous Diamond Swindle. Two prospectors arrived in San Francisco claiming to have found diamond mines worth millions of dollars. They led an eager and credulous group of potential investors to a pre-arranged site that had been "salted." After diamonds appeared in soil samples (previously purchased abroad by the swindlers for between $30,000 and $40,000), several very respectable financiers formed an investment syndicate that bought out the promoters for $600,000.

By some shrewd detective work, Wilson and his companions established that the alleged mines would have been in territory examined that very summer by the Fortieth Parallel Survey. "Put on their mettle," as Wilson said, to suppose that such riches had been found under the noses of seasoned geologists by a couple of lucky prospectors, they secretly returned to the

121

field. Wilson, King, and Emmons found a site staked out, complete with a sprinkling of diamonds, in the northwest corner of Colorado. They spent the next two days systematically examining the ground and testing the soil, after which they concluded that a terrible fraud had been created. They returned immediately by train to San Francisco with their evidence, exposed the unhappy details, and saved further loss by fresh investors. The original syndicate swallowed more than pride, but did pay off the other investors and absorbed the loss.[8]

King finished his field work after the 1872 season and spent the next several years preparing his results for publication. Wilson wanted to stay in the field. The result was that both he and J.T. Gardner transferred to Ferdinand V. Hayden's U.S. Geological and Geographical Survey of the Territories, Gardner becoming geographer and Wilson leader of the party that pioneered the exploration of southern and southwestern Colorado in 1873–75.

His new colleagues thought as highly of him as his old comrades had. George B. Chittenden, assistant topographer to Wilson during the 1873 season, wrote his mother that "Wilson is a first-rate topographer and as a mountaineer has few equals in the country. His knowledge of the mountains amounts almost to instinct and astonishes me."[9] The geologist who accompanied Wilson for three seasons in Colorado, Fred Endlich, also praised him in a letter to Hayden.

> Mr. Wilson, as you undoubtedly know, is one of the best workers imaginable, and does his work in the most careful way. I think you can promise yourself the best results from his industrious energy.

In his report for the 1874 season Endlich credited Wilson for a sharp geological eye; on one occasion he had identified the outcrop of an important quartzite formation, and on another he had located an unnoticed bed of coal.[10]

Rhoda served his apprenticeship under his half brother during the same three years, beginning as "computer" and moving up to assistant topographer. Near the end of their third season together, the same G.B. Chittenden reported to Hayden that

"Wilson wrote me a note which reached me at Denver. He and Rhoda are evidently both making stations and getting along wonderfully."[11] This testifies to their enduring bond as brothers, and to the expertise Rhoda had gained, for in addition to making profile and drainage sketches, doing mathematical computations for the triangulation, and writing up the results, Rhoda had apparently earned the right to make stations on his own. Under Wilson's tutelage he had become in fact, if not in name, a full-fledged topographer.

After the third season in Colorado, J.T. Gardner departed and Wilson took over as geographer, with responsibility for the primary triangulation of the Hayden Survey. In 1876 he completed the groundwork laid by Gardner for Colorado, and he drew the final maps which appeared the following year in the resplendent and highly acclaimed *Atlas of Colorado.*

During the 1877 and 1878 seasons he did the primary triangulation in western Wyoming and eastern Idaho. The stations he established linked directly with those he had made for King in 1871 and 1872. His surveying took him through the Wind River, Grosventre, Wyoming, and Teton Ranges, where he added more first ascents to his already impressive list.

Not all the drama of frontier exploration was in Colorado, as Wilson's reports show. On August 24, 1878 his party made camp beneath Sawtell Peak, near Henry's Lake in Idaho.

> After dinner we were lying about the fire, smoking and talking, when suddenly, all unconscious of any approaching danger, some shots were fired just behind us, and as quick as a flash we all dropped to our hands and feet and crawled for our rifles, some one calling out "Indians." Just as I picked up my rifle I heard our stock start off on the run. I knew at once that we were left on foot beyond all redemption, as the Indians were on horseback and already had the start of us.

As it was already dark, the Indians contented themselves with firing occasional shots and surrounding the party. Obviously, they would make a move in the morning. Wilson "determined to crawl out to some woods, where my little party of five, with our four guns, might stand a better chance if they should find us."[12] His years of experience in the wilderness undoubtedly saved the party. Having cached their instruments and most of the supplies, they snaked their way past the Indians, and after a three-day march with limited supplies found Hayden's party at the Upper Geyser Basin. Next morning, furious at being outsmarted, the Indians destroyed the campsite and everything they could find. Wilson returned days later to retrieve the valuable instruments the Indians had not discovered.

In 1879 Hayden's Survey was merged with the others that had been operating on an autonomous basis to form the United States Geological Survey. On July 10 Wilson was appointed chief topographer. His first assignment was to join his old friend S.F. Emmons in a survey of the Leadville, Colorado area. He spent two seasons in the field preparing the maps for Emmons' report, which covered Leadville and the nearby Mosquito Range.[13]

Wilson resigned from the USGS on September 30, 1881 in order to become topographer for the Northern Transcontinental Survey, organized by Raphael Pumpelly. Henry Villard, president of the Northern Pacific Railroad, had invited Pumpelly to map the sprawling areas of Washington, Idaho, and Montana embraced by his ambitious railroad empire, and to identify the economic resources near the several lines he controlled. The party stayed together through the winter of 1884, though field work stopped after the 1883 season because the parent company was derailed by reorganization problems and the survey abandoned.[14]

Because of his wide experience in Colorado and his outstanding reputation, no one was surprised when in 1885 the General Land Office called on Wilson to settle a dispute about Colorado's western border, the 109th meridian. Rollin Reeves had done the official survey in 1878, but apparently due to bad weather Reeves was unable to take observations on Polaris for eleven nights to keep him on a true north course. Thus he strayed some seven degrees too far west for nearly eight miles, the result being that Colorado expropriated a piece of Utah. Wilson's resurvey of part of the 109th meridian confirmed the error, but since Reeves' was the official survey, the border remained and remains unchanged.[15]

Over the next decade Wilson reoriented himself to home

base, Oakland, and began shifting his interests from surveying to local business. Actually, one led to the other. The Western Pacific Railroad hired him to find a line from Salt Lake City to Oakland via Beckwourth Pass in the Sierra Nevada.[16] In doing so, he relied largely on his earlier work with Clarence King over much of the same territory. Later Wilson surveyed a line from Stockton to Oakland and assisted the railroad in gaining its right of way into Oakland.[17]

On March 3, 1903 several business leaders in Oakland, including Wilson, organized The Athenian Bank. On October 22 of that year they changed its name to Security Bank and Trust of Oakland and appointed Wilson a director and vice president. He held both positions until his retirement on March 3, 1914. Thereafter he served on the board of directors until the Bank of Italy absorbed the bank in 1918. From then until his death he served on an advisory committee for the Bank of Italy that supervised business development at the Oakland Branch.[18]

Deliberate and circumspect in all aspects of his career, Wilson also exercised prudence in important aspects of his private life. He married only in 1895, at the age of 50 or 51. Amelia Stevens was the daughter of a prominnt Oakland pioneer who had built a substantial shipping business. Coincidentally, she was the same "Kitty" Stevens who fifteen years before had assisted her husband's halfbrother in starting the first Sunday school in Fruitvale.[19]

Wilson applied good judgment to his business affairs too. Beginning with a sizable parcel of land obtained from his stepfather, he added other real estate and investments so that he died a wealthy man, unlike the less frugal Rhoda, who had started with similar resources.

The contrast between the two brothers was pronounced, and it extended beyond careers: divergent attitudes about the material world, varying social values, spiritual manifestations, literary and artistic appreciations. Yet their differences did not separate them. Mutual interests in the outdoors and surveying that had developed during the Colorado years persisted and kept them close. In the summer of 1907 Wilson invited Rhoda to take a vacation with him to Yellowstone National Park, at his expense. Rhoda accepted, and they were together for a month.[20]

"Uncle Wilson" always displayed affection and warmth for Rhoda's children, all nine of them. He never had any of his own. After his death, it was discovered that while he had left the bulk of his estate to his wife, he had also provided Rhoda an annuity of $50 a month (half his former pastor's salary) and a moderate trust that would distribute upon Amelia's death to Rhoda's surviving children. Amelia paid the annuity for the duration of Rhoda's life, and at her death in 1932 each of the children received their distributions.

Wilson died of influenza on February 21, 1920, at the age of seventy-five. Nine and a half years later, Rhoda died, also at the age of seventy-five.

Notes

1. Rev. Franklin Rhoda, "Auto-Biographical Sketch," a type-script written June 29, 1922, in Point Arena, California; John Rhoda, "Frederick Rhoda," a typescript written some time after 1959. The former exists in the Library of the California Historical Society. The latter is among the private papers of Rhoda's granddaughter, Pauline Vieira (Mrs. Gerald J. Vieira). John Rhoda was the grandson of Frederick Rhoda and the son of Franklin.

2. Ellis A. Davis, *Davis' Commercial Encyclopedia of the Pacific Southwest* (Berkeley, 1914), p. 236.

3. Samuel Willey, *A History of the College of California* (San Francisco, 1887), especially pp. 54–58, 73, 106–107, 165, 245–47.

4. J.D. Whitney, *Letter of the State Geologist, Relative to the Progress of the State Geological Survey, During the Years 1866–67* (Sacramento, 1867), p. 6

5. Edwin Tenney Brewster, *Life and Letters of Josiah Dwight Whitney* (Boston, 1909), p. 265.

6. Clarence King, "Letters to Brig. Genl. A.A. Humphreys, 1867–78," National Archives, Record Group 57, Microcopy 622/Roll 3, letter of July 10, 1868.

7. Dee Molenaar, "The Climbing History of Mount Ranier," *American Alpine Journal*, Vol. X, No. 2 (1957).

8. Allen D. Wilson, "The Great California Diamond Mines: A True Story," *Overland Monthly*, Vol. XLIII, No. 4 (April 1904).

9. Letter of July 28, Chittenden Letters, Denver Public Library.

10. Letter of August 1, 1873, National Archives, Record Group 57, Microcopy 623/Roll 3; F.V. Hayden, *Eighth Annual Report of the United States Geological and Geographical Survey of the Territories* (Washington, 1876), pp. 188 & 226.

11. Letter of September 28, 1875, National Archives, Record Group 57, Microcopy 623/Roll 6.

12. F.V. Hayden, *Eleventh Annual Report of the United States Geological and Geographical Survey of the Territories* (Washington, 1879), p. 659.

13. S.F. Emmons, *Geology and Mining Industry of Leadville, Colorado,* which is Vol. XII of *Monographs of the USGS* (Washington, 1886), p. viii.

14. Raphael Pumpelly, *My Reminiscences* (New York, 1918), II, 624–28; Bailey Willis, *Biographical Memoir of Raphael Pumpelly, 1837–1923,* Vol. XVI of *Biographical Memoires,* published by the National Academy of Sciences (Washington, 1936), p. 52.

15. "Survey Error Gave Colorado Hundred-Mile Chunk of Utah," *The Denver Post,* March 16, 1958, page 2A; National Archives, Laura E. Kelsay, compiler, *List of Cartographic Records of the General Land Office (Record Group 49)* (Washington, 1964), p. 93.

16. Not Beckwith Pass, as the source in note 2 above says. Lt. E.G. Beckwith found some passes across the Sierra Nevada while working on the Pacific Railroad Survey in the 1850s, but this pass was discovered in 1850 by James P. Beckwourth, the famous black mountain man.

17. See note 2 above.

18. Minute Book, Board of Directors, Security Bank of Oakland; Minute Book for Oakland Branch Advisory Committee, Bank of Italy; "Bank of Italy Enters Oakland," *BankItaly Life,* Vol. II, No. 11 (November, 1918). I am grateful to Teresa Hickey, Archivist for the Bank of America, for providing this information, and to Patrick Carroll, California Banking Commission, San Francisco, who confirmed Wilson's connection with The Athenian Bank from the *Annual Reports of the Superintendent of Banks.*

19. Fruitvale Presbyterian Church, Oakland, Session Book One, "History of Fruitvale Presbyterian Church," facing page 1.

20. *Ibid.,* p. 124.

Frederick M. Endlich. *From an 1899 edition of Engineering & Mining Journal.*

FRED ENDLICH

The third of the trio, Frederick Miller Endlich, appears in several ways as the man in the middle. Viewed in retrospect, Endlich was neither as versatile as Rhoda nor as materially successful as Wilson. On the other hand, during his shorter life he attained a wider reputation than either, and he avoided the ideological extremism of Rhoda and the comfortable obscurity of Wilson.

Coincidentally, Endlich and Rhoda shared the same birthday, June 14. Endlich was born three years earlier, in 1851, in Reading, Pennsylvania. Therefore he was twenty-two in the summer of 1873, the year he and Rhoda and Wilson each began working for Hayden. Rhoda was just nineteen, Wilson twenty-nine.

The most cosmopolitan of the three, Endlich traveled extensively during his life, beginning at age six when he went with his father to live for four years in Switzerland. His father was United States Consul, 1857–61, stationed in Basel, which suggests the family had means and political connections.[1]

Returning to Europe in 1866, he studied there for four years, first at the Polytechnic Institute in Stuttgart, then at the University of Tubingen, where he obtained the doctorate in natural sciences. His generation was the first in America to gain much formal graduate education in geology and paleontology. Hayden, for example, typical of his generation (he was forty-six in 1873), earned an M.D. and learned most of his geology in the field. The earliest American scientific schools, like Sheffield at Yale or Lawrence at Harvard, were only just coming into their own by the middle 1860s, and students of such relatively new disciplines as geology often pursued advanced training abroad. Endlich was not unique in this. Arnold Hague and S.F. Emmons (King's geologists), to mention just two, also studied in Europe.

Endlich returned to Germany for another year to work at the University of Breslau and in Freiberg, the latter boasting the most renowned mining academy of the time. All the training paid off, for he caught the attention of the Smithsonian Institution. Between its director and secretary, Joseph Henry, and its assistant secretary, Spencer Fullerton Baird, the Smithsonian had ties to virtually every American scientist of standing. Baird, incidentally, had also been born in Reading, Pennsylvania. In 1872 the Smithsonian hired Endlich as a mineralogist, geologist, chemist, and mining expert, a position he retained until 1880.

Between 1873 and 1879 Endlich worked with the Hayden Survey as well, gaining valuable field experience and contributing significantly to Hayden's reports on geology and mineral resources in the Rocky Mountains. Endlich's close collaboration with Rhoda and Wilson over three consecutive years typified the cooperation that produced the *Atlas of Colorado*.

> The method of working I have arranged so as to coincide as nearly as possible with the topographical work. My notes and sketches progress step for step with Mr. Wilson's topographical contours, and I accompany him wherever he goes. In order to be able to correctly color (as far as possible in a short time) the future geological map, I have made a great number of both local and continuous sections. In work that I have formerly done, I have found these sections to be of great value and where we have no maps at hand, when identified with the topographical work, they will greatly facilitate the final report upon the geology of some section of the country.[2]

Perhaps reflecting his Germanic training, Endlich was a punctilious worker, and, with some notable exceptions, a model of deference. Hayden requested frequent reports from all his professionals, but Wilson and Rhoda never wrote Hayden during this period (Rhoda did write once to his assistant), while Endlich sent scores of detailed letters from the field. It is these letters that give us an impression of the man.

Nothing if not orderly, Endlich, like others blessed with methodical competence, may have looked down somewhat on lesser mortals. In submitting his 1874 report to Hayden his anxiety about its correct reproduction caused him to forget he was writing his boss, who would edit all the reports into a final annual report. "You will also find instructions for the 'editor of the report' where everything is carefully detailed, so that no misunderstanding can possibly occur . . . I have written explicit instructions about it . . . With the arrangement and instructions as given, I do not think that any mistakes can occur."[3]

Such tightly coiled tidiness could be wound up to a high dudgeon. James T. Gardner wrote a report on coal deposits that lay in the region explored by Endlich during 1875. Endlich wrote Hayden on August 31:

> It will scarcely surprise you when I say that at very least I was astonished to find that Mr. G. who certainly never has published any work on geology, undertook to examine and report upon a section of country that was assigned to me for investigation. I assume that it was done without direct orders from yourself, else Mr. G. would certainly not have proceeded in the way he did—by stealth—and you would probably have acquainted me with the fact. It is very apparent, from the report itself, that the examinations were not made purely for the sake of scientific truth, but more likely to further the interests of some corporation, with which I do not happen to be acquainted. As geologist of the southern division, carrying out the work as directed by yourself, I can not otherwise regard such proceedings than as wanton interference, if not more selfish considerations underlie. This all is solely under the assumption that no such examinations by Mr. G was [sic] directly ordered by yourself.

Whatever he may have thought, Hayden replied that he too was surprised at Gardner's pamphlet. This was the second headache Gardner had caused Hayden in 1875. Gardner's party had been ambushed by Indians, and Hayden was distressed at the way events transpired, especially the abandoning of valuable instruments and supplies. In the end Gardner got the sack, which led to Wilson taking over as geographer. Upon hearing the news, Endlich wrote on October 30, gloating, "The news regarding Mr. G is very gratifying, it will no doubt save you much annoyance and trouble, and be better for your survey." The next season Endlich geologized in the White River region of Colorado, and during the following season in the Sweetwater district of Wyoming.

All the men who worked for him seemed to agree that Hayden was an exacting taskmaster, but one they would follow through fire, because of his loyal support of them. With his letter of February 3, 1877 Endlich displayed a surprising annoyance, bordering on insubordination.

Dear Sir,

I have received your note of this morning. In explanation of my not having been at your office yesterday, I wish to say, that both maps upon which I am at work were in the hands of other geologists, at the time of my leaving Friday. Furthermore, I was absolutely prevented from being there yesterday morning, and the afternoon was certainly devoted to your service, if even not at the office.

So far as the regular hours are concerned, I beg leave to state my regret at the utter impossibility to keep them, and would remind you of the fact that no regular hours have ever been agreed upon between us. On the other hand, I am very willing to guarantee to you the completion of both maps and reports at the same average time that they will be completed by your other geologists, or at any given date that you may set for them and me.

I am sorry that you considered it necessary to appoint definite hours of work, and would ask that you give me my own time for the completion of both maps and reports in accordance with the suggestion above.

Very truly yours,

Fred'c M Endlich

Endlich had been ill that winter; perhaps that explains his unwillingness to keep definite hours. His letters to Hayden dropped off for a while. Apparently no breach occurred, however, for they resume and give a summary of the field work of 1877 and conclude with one on October 14 enclosing a present for Mrs. Hayden of some mineralogical specimens that he considered superior.

Endlich was a proud man, and a part of that pride derived from his work. On January 21, 1878 he wrote Hayden, "Together with this I send you the manuscript of the mineral catalogue. I have been to Philadelphia and finished it. I have 200 species, over 800 localities and nearly 40 analyses in it. It is the most complete thing in the way of a mineral-list published about any state in the U.S." Hayden would have understood that kind of pride, for he possessed the same in abundance.

But Endlich had pride of another kind, too, pride of social place. After all, he was the son of a consul, and he had the finest education a scientist could find. He was on friendly terms with influential people, among them Congressman Hiester Clymer, who sat on the Appropriations Committee of the House. Endlich also had a competitive flair and loved a good fight. He took pleasure in the rivalry for funds that existed with the other surveys, and he cheered Hayden on from the sidelines.

On November 16, 1878 he was one of the select few invited by J.W. Powell to his home in Washington to assist at the creation of the Cosmos Club. Others attending included the literary lion, Henry Adams, and Powell's own geologist, Clarence Dutton. The club was a gathering place for the self-proclaimed leaders of Washington's scientific and intellectual circle.[4] It was probably because of such connections that Endlich carried an ambivalent attitude to the lowlyborn and mostly self-educated Hayden. Powell was also lowlyborn and mostly self-educated, though he fared better than Hayden in the struggle for political position, and he was the toast of Washington in the 1880s. Endlich was to turn on Powell with a bitterness he never showed Hayden. And all because of a kindred spirit of gentle birth who also loved a fight, Edward Drinker Cope.

As a paleontologist, Cope was a good collector and a prolific if hasty writer, and most of his findings reached the world through one of Hayden's publications. Cope had lots of enemies. Othniel Charles Marsh was his professional rival, for they had crossed swords in the fossil-rich trenches of the West. J.W. Powell was a political opponent because he would not assist Cope to a government job or publish his work. In 1884 Congress began sniffing around for ways of cutting costs in governmental projects, as was its wont periodically. At the time Powell was director of the USGS and chief of the Bureau of Ethnology. Marsh was paleontologist for the USGS and president of the National Academy of Sciences. Each had a big thumb in the pie of scientific-political influence.

Nothing daunted, Cope launched an attack on the wastefulness of the USGS, and continued his personal feud with Marsh. Endlich, who by now participated in mining enterprises with Cope, was enlisted to gather evidence from some of his former associates in the Hayden Survey who now served under Powell. The scheme backfired when his erstwhile chums turned his letters over to Powell, who was able to make a convincing case of sour grapes against Endlich and Cope. Congress overlooked Copes's charges and ended by endorsing Powell. Endlich, doubtless embarrassed, withdrew from the conflict. Cope carried it on, with results that continued to embarrass Endlich.[5]

When Hayden's Survey disintegrated in 1879 Endlich still had a position with the Smithsonian, but he needed more than that. The next few years are well summarized in his obituary.

> In 1880 Dr. Endlich was appointed general manager of the Grand View Mine at Rico, Colorado, his first work being to build the smelting works at Rico. For the next ten years he was employed in opening and managing mines, his charges including the Lake Valley [also known as the Sierra Mining Companies] and San Pedro mines in New Mexico, the Santa Rita in Arizona, the Grand View and Yankee Boy in Colorado. During this period also he visited Nova Scotia professionally, and made a trip to the West Indies and South America for the United States Government to investigate the artificial coloration of sugar. He opened the San Xavier Mine near Tucson, Arizona, and several mines near Socorro in New Mexico. He designed and built many important mills and reduction works, including the first large leaching mill for the Russell process.
>
> Some years ago, after leaving Colorado about 1893, Dr. Endlich settled in Los Angeles, California, opening an office as a consulting engineer. His work was largely in Southern California and Arizona.[6]

In the 1890s he also was associated with the Saginaw Copper Mining Company, then later with the Martinique Copper Company, both in Arizona.[7] He lived in Tucson for the last year or so of his life. His end came suddenly and tragically. Apparently down on his luck, he borrowed a 41 caliber revolver from a friend at the Orndorff Hotel and shot himself.[8] Though married, he and his wife had been separated for some time.

Perhaps the best brief measure of his career would be a review of his writings. He managed to publish at least one study on each of the several regions he explored personally, including parts of New Mexico, Arizona, Southern California, Colorado, Wyoming, and the island of Dominica in the Caribbean Sea.[9] He excelled in drafting concise statements on the physical geology of a locality. His particular interests in mineralogy and economic geology led him to specialize in mining engineering. His most influential publication, *Manual of Qualitative Blowpipe Analysis and Determinative Mineralogy* (1892), provided an encyclopedic approach to a technical subject and contributed original comments based on his own experience. His articles appeared in leading scientific journals of the day, including the *Bulletin of the Philosophic Society of Washington* and *The Engineering and Mining Journal.* An ungenerous critic might quibble that two of his pieces appeared in the *American Naturalist*, which was then owned by his friend and business associate, E.D. Cope. On the other hand, *The American Journal of Science and Arts* published at least two of his essays also, and it was edited in New Haven by men friendly to O.C. Marsh, the archenemy of Cope. Scientists at least regarded Endlich's contributions impartially.

At least most of them did. Commenting on the maps produced by Hayden's geologists in Colorado, S.F. Emmons, Wilson's longtime colleague, praised "the substantial accuracy of the geological outlines laid down on these maps, except in southeastern Colorado and in the San Juan mountains, where at the various points examined the facts of nature show such wide divergence from these outlines, as laid down by Mr. Endlich, as to throw serious discredit upon all of his field work."[10] Emmons' criticism is so sweeping as to arouse suspicion, especially since Endlich's field techniques followed the standards of other geologists working with him in Colorado. Emmons may have regarded the attacks of 1884–85 by Endlich and Cope on the USGS as in part a personal attack on him, since he was a prominent personage at the USGS during those years. Interestingly, Emmons published his hostile remarks in 1890, the year the battle between Cope and Powell reached its peak with the appearance of a series of articles in the *New York Herald*. Endlich had withdrawn from the conflict by then, but in the eyes of the Washington elite he was still remembered as Cope's ally and a man who had betrayed Powell.

A fairer appraisal of Endlich's work in Colorado came a few years later by men who had no ax to grind. Writing in *The Proceedings of the Colorado Scientific Society*, they pointed out the general value of Hayden's geological maps, and they added corrections based upon more detailed surveys than the rapid (and pioneering) pace of Hayden's men would permit.[11]

This short summary of Endlich's life is not the place to resolve his status as a scientist. One other original contribution deserves mention, however. In the 1870s a war of words ensued over the correct age of the lignitic coal beds of the West. Some scholars said Cretaceous, others Tertiary. Hayden commented that the problems arose largely because of trying to adapt European periodization too rigidly to American circumstances, which, despite general similarities, disclosed unique differences.[12] Hayden later made refinements in the stratigraphic column of North America, but as early as 1875 Endlich had anticipated that step in a letter to Hayden, which said, "so far as I can determine, the lignitic group can certainly not be counted to the Cretaceous, but is a transitory one between that and the Tertiary."[13]

Whatever the ultimate decision on his scientific contributions, it seems appropriate that his work in mineralogy has been immortalized.

Endlichite: a mineral in composition falling between mimetite and vanadinite and consisting of lead arsenate, vanadate, and chloride.

Webster's Third New International Dictionary

Notes

1. Obituary in *The Engineering and Mining Journal*, July 29, 1899, page 126.

2. Letter to F.V. Hayden, August 1, 1873. This and the letters mentioned below are in the National Archives, Record Group 57, and were read on Microcopy 623/Rolls 3 & 7.

3. Letter to Hayden, May 26, 1875.

4. Wallace Stegner, *Beyond the Hundreth Meridian* (Lincoln, 1982), pp. 242 & 404.

5. Elizabeth Nobel Shor, *The Fossil Feud Between E.D. Cope and O.C. Marsh* (Hicksville, N.Y., 1974) quotes Endlich's letters on behalf of Cope, pp. 94–96. Henry F. Osborn, *Cope: Master Naturalist* (Princeton, 1931) documents the business connections, pp. 286–91.

6. See note 1 above.

7. Obituaries in the *Arizona Daily Citizen*, July 17, 1899, page 4; and *Arizona Daily Star*, July 18, 1899, page 1.

8. *Ibid.*

9. Most of his writings are mentioned in John M. Nickles, *Geologic Literature on North America, 1785–1918* (USGS Bulletins 746–747, 1923), but not the articles in *The American Journal of Science and Arts*.

10. "Orographic Movements in the Rocky Mountains," *Bulletin of the Geological Society of America*, I (1890), p. 249.

11. See Vol. V (1894–96), pp. 25 & 76-77.

12. *Ninth Annual Report of the United States Geological and Geographical Survey of the Territories* (Washington, 1877), pp. 20–21.

13. Letter of October 4, 1875.

APPENDIX
List and Location of Stations

One finds most of the stations without difficulty on either the "Preliminary Map" of 1874, published with Hayden's annual report for that year, or Hayden's *Atlas of Colorado* (1881 ed.), the Survey's final depiction of four years' work. As a check, I also used Rhoda's tables (not reprinted in this edition) that show elevation, longitude, and latitude of numerous points. His numbers vary from modern standards but so slightly that when transposed to recent maps they locate most stations readily. Station 50 appears on none of these sources, but I found it on the original hand-drawn composite map of the many field sketches (see note 83 to the text). As a final check, I used Rhoda's text while in the field to confirm the chosen sites.

Use the County Map Series to locate the stations. Visualize each map divided into quarters, numbered clockwise from the upper right quadrant (1st) through the upper left (4th). Thus, the reference for Agency Peak, Saguache 1:3, tells you to look on Sheet 1 of the Saguache County Maps in the third quadrant (lower left).

An asterisk * means access via private property.

Station	Modern Elevation	Geographic or Station name	Map Location
1	11,719	Agency Peak	Saguache 1:3
2	13,502		Hinsdale 1:2 ENE of Baldy Cinco
3	12,644	Cannibal	Hinsdale 1:1
4	11,876		Gunnison 6:2 S of Cap Mountain
5	12,800	Lake	Hinsdale 1:1
6	9,940	Rudolph	Gunnison 6:2 N of Rudolph Hill
7*	9,029	Cap Mountain	Gunnison 6:2
8	12,933	Crystal Peak	Hinsdale 1:4
9	14,309	Uncompahgre Peak	Hinsdale 1:4
10	13,132		Ouray 2:2 N of Engineer Pass
11	10,726	Station Eleven	Hinsdale 1:1

12	14,001	Sunshine Peak	Hinsdale 1:3
13	12,720		Hinsdale 1:3 Between Stations 12 & 14
14	14,048	Handies Peak	Hinsdale 1:3
15	13,722		San Juan 1:1 NW of Cinnamon Pass
16	13,552	Tower Mountain	San Juan 1:1
17	12,880		San Juan 1:2 E of Highland Mary Lakes just W of Continental Divide
18	13,716	Pole Creek Mountain	Hinsdale 2:4
19	12,258	Finger Mesa	Hinsdale 2:4
20	12,258	Finger Mesa	Hinsdale 2:4
21	13,821	Rio Grande Pyramid	Hinsdale 2:4
22	12,960		Hinsdale 2:3 S of Mesa Lato
23	13,684	Mt. Oso	La Plata 1:1
24	12,800		San Juan 1:2 Just SE of Hunchback Pass
25	13,627	White Dome	San Juan 1:2
26	13,368	Sultan Mountain	San Juan 1:1–2
27	12,673	Ohio peak	San Juan 1:1
28	12,890	Red Mountain No. 3	San Juan 1:1
29	13,206		Ouray 2:2 Just N of Richmond Pass
30	13,894	Vermillion Peak	San Juan 1:4
31	12,968	Engineer Mountain	San Juan 1:3
32	8,880		San Miguel 3:1–2 Just W of Keystone
33	14,150	Mt. Sneffels	Ouray 2:4
34	12,987	Hayden Peak	San Miguel 3:1
35	14,246	Mount Wilson	Dolores 3:1
36	12,579	Hermosa Peak	Dolores 3:2
37	12,681	Blackhawk Mountain	Dolores 3:2
38	13,077	Snowdon Peak	San Juan 1:2
39	10,532	Hermosa Cliffs	La Plata 1:4
40	8,885		La Plata 3:4 E of Trimble
41	8,320	Perins Peak	La Plata 3:4
42	10,664	Sliderock Mountain	La Plata 3:4
43	10,720	Sliderock Mountain	La Plata 2:1
44*	8,175		La Plata 3:4 E of Horse Gulch
45*	8,260		La Plata 2:2 E of Breen
46*	6,880		La Plata 3:4 Ridge E of Durango near Golf Range

47*	8,892	Vosburg Pike	La Plata 3:1
48	12,311	Crevasse	La Plata 1:2
49	11,740	Miller Mountain	La Plata 1:2
50	12,147	Granite Peak	Hinsdale 2:3 E of Runlett Peak *not* the Granite Peak N of Divide Lakes
51	12,531	Graham Peak	Hinsdale 2:3
52	11,006		Hinsdale 2:3 S of Divide Lakes
53	10,852	Park	Hinsdale 2:1 NE of River Hill Campground
54*	12,706	Bristol Head	Mineral 1:3

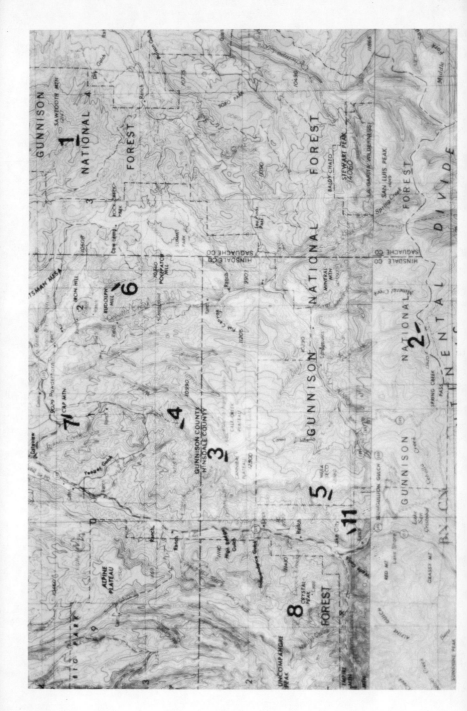

145

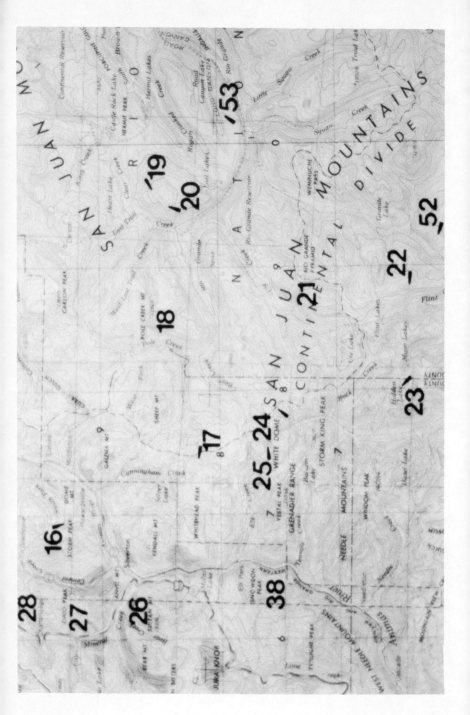

146

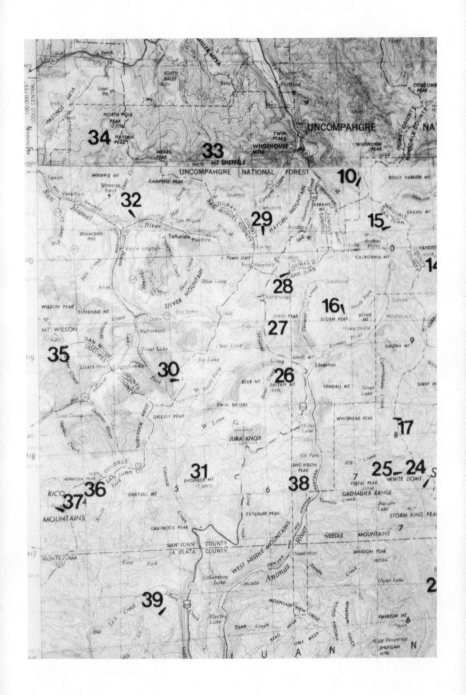

147

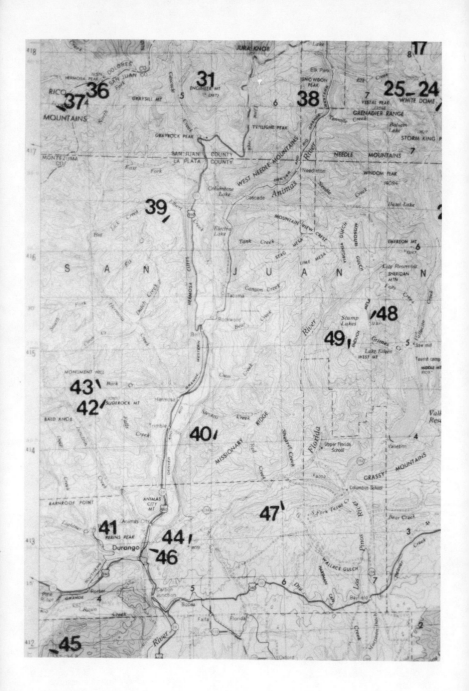

148

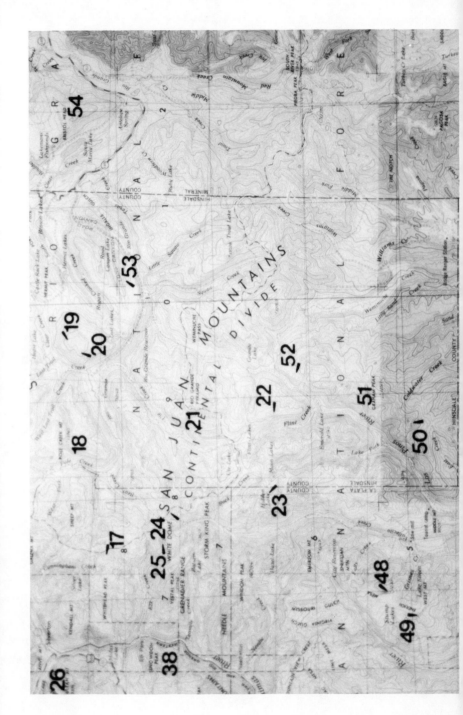

149

FURTHER READING

Richard A. Bartlett, *Great Surveys of the American West*. Norman: University of Oklahoma Press, 1962.

Margaret Bates, *A Quick History of Lake City Colorado*. Colorado Springs: Little London press, 1973.

Jack L. Benham, *Silverton and Neighboring Ghost Towns*. Ouray: Bear Creek Publishing Co., 1981.

Colorado Geographic Names: Alphabetical Finding List, compiled by Branch of Geographic Names, USGS. Reston, Virginia: USGS, 1981.

Colorado: A Guide to the Highest State, compiled by Work Projects Administration. New York: Hastings House, 1941.

William H. Goetzmann, *Exploration and Empire*. New York: W.W. Norton & Co., 1966.

Robert P. Larkin, and others, *The Southern Rocky Mountains*, K/H Geology Field Guide Series. Dubuque, Iowa: Kendall/Hunt Publishing Co., 1980.

Ernest Ingersoll, *Silver San Juan* [1882]. Olympic Valley, California: Outbooks, 1977.

Mary C. Rabbitt, *Minerals, Lands, and Geology for the Common Defence and General Welfare*, Volume I. Washington: US Government Printing Office, 1979.

Marshall Sprague, *The Great Gates*. Boston: Little, Brown & Co., 1964.

Duane Vandenbusche and Duane A. Smith, *A Land Alone: Colorado's Western Slope*. Boulder: Pruett Publishing Co., 1981.

Muriel Sibell Wolle, *Stampede to Timberline*. Chicago: The Swallow Press, 1974

INDEX

Mike Foster was born in Denver to a family whose last four generations have grown up in Colorado. A professional historian and amateur naturalist, he enjoys climbing mountains and studying the West's early explorers. Foster currently lives in Denver, where he is at work on several other projects relating to the exploration of Colorado and the West.